And as I Rode by Granard Moat

Benedict Kiely

THE LILLIPUT PRESS
DUBLIN

First published in 1996 by
THE LILLIPUT PRESS LTD
4 Rosemount Terrace, Arbour Hill,
Dublin 7, Ireland.

A CIP record for this
title is available from
The British Library.

ISBN 0 946640 78 5 (PBK)

Cover design by Jarlath Hayes
Set in Bembo
Printed in Ireland by
Betaprint of Dublin

AND AS I RODE BY GRANARD MOAT

For Ciarán MacMathúna
who owns the world that I wandered through

Contents

Preface 1

I Ulster 5

'The Green Flowery Banks' [Anon.] 7; 'The Ballad of Douglas Bridge'
[Francis Carlin] 9; 'Me an' Me Da' [Rev. Marshall] 10; 'When I Was a
Little Girl' [Alice Milligan] 12; 'The Ould Orange Flute' [Anon.] 14;
'The Hills above Drumquin' [Felix Kearney] 16; 'Drumquin Creamery'
[Anon.] 17; 'The Man from God Knows Where' [Florence Wilson] 19;
'Old Ardboe' [Anon.] 23; 'Lament for Thomas Davis' [Samuel Ferguson]
25; ''Tis Pretty tae be in Baile-liosan' [Joseph Campbell] 27; 'Sweet
Omagh Town' [Anon.] 28; 'The Treacherous Waves of Loughmuck'
[Frank McCrory] 29; 'Song of the Little Villages' [James Dollard] 31;
'The Winding Banks of Erne' [William Allingham] 33; 'The Pilgrim'
[W.B. Yeats] 36; 'The Lough Derg Pilgrim' [Seamus Heaney] 37; 'Like
Dolmens Round My Childhood, the Old People' [John Montague] 39;
'A Lost Tradition' [John Montague] 40; 'Lough Erne Shore' [Anon.] 42;
'The Maid of Lough Gowna Shore' [Anon.] 43; 'The Mantle So Green'
[Anon.] 45; 'Nell Flaherty's Drake' [Percy French] 49; 'O'Hussey's Ode
to the Maguire' [James Clarence Mangan] 50; 'The Wake of William
Orr' [William Drennan] 53; 'The Maiden City' [Charlotte Elizabeth] 54;
'Aodh Ruadh Ó Domhnaill' [Thomas MacGreevy] 56; 'The Forsaken
Soldier' [Hudie Devaney, tr. Paddy Tunney] 57; 'A Christmas Child-
hood' [Patrick Kavanagh] 58; 'Deirdre' [James Stephens] 60; 'The Lions
of the Hill Are Gone' [Samuel Ferguson] 61; 'Lent' [W.R. Rodgers] 63;
'I Am the Mountainy Singer' [Joseph Campbell] 65; 'Ballad to a
Traditional Refrain' [Maurice Craig] 66; 'Sarah Ann' [Rev. Marshall] 66;
'The Runaway' [Rev. Marshall] 68; 'The Boys of Mullaghbawn' [Anon.]
72; 'Wild Slieve Gallen Brae' [David Hammond] 73

II From Ulster to Leinster 75

'Boyne Water' [Anon.] 75; 'Train to Dublin' [Louis MacNeice] 78; 'Dublin' [Louis MacNeice] 79; 'The Humours of Donnybrook Fair' [Anon.] 81; 'Dublin Made Me' [Donagh MacDonagh] 83; 'Down by the Liffey Side' [Donagh MacDonagh] 84; 'Autumn Afternoon' [Roibeard Ó Faracháin] 86; 'Dublin's Children' [Padraic Gregory] 88; 'The Hill of Killenarden' [Charles Halpine] 89; 'She Walked Unaware' [Patrick MacDonogh] 90; 'Mary Hynes' [Padraic Fallon, after Raftery] 91; 'The Western World' [Robert Farren] 94; 'Spraying the Potatoes' [Patrick Kavanagh] 95; 'Renewal' [Patrick Kavanagh] 96; 'Spring Stops Me Suddenly' [Valentin Iremonger] 97; 'A Racehorse at the Curragh' [Francis Stuart] 98; 'My Love Is like the Sun' [Anon.] 99; 'Bellewstown Hill' [John Costello] 100; 'The Night before Larry was Stretched' [attd to Rev. Robt Burrowes] 102; 'The Boyne Walk' [F.R. Higgins] 105; 'On Seeing Swift in Laracor' [Brinsley MacNamara] 108; 'Going to Mass Last Sunday' [Donagh MacDonagh] 109; 'The Yellow Bittern' [C.B. Mac Giolla Gunna, tr. Thomas MacDonagh] 110; 'Padraic O'Conaire – Gaelic Storyteller' [F. R. Higgins] 111; 'Georgian Dublin' [Maurice Craig] 113; 'An Elegy on the Death of a Mad Dog' [Oliver Goldsmith] 113; 'Twenty Golden Years Ago' [James Clarence Mangan] 115; 'The Time of the Barmecides' [James Clarence Mangan] 117; 'The Woman of Three Cows' [Anon., tr. James Clarence Mangan] 119; 'Gone in the Wind' [James Clarence Mangan] 120; 'King Brian before the Battle' [William Kennelly] 122; 'Lament for Dædalus' [John Sterling] 123; 'Leda and the Swan' [Oliver St John Gogarty] 125; 'Canal Bank Walk' [Patrick Kavanagh] 129; 'Lines Written on a Seat on the Grand Canal' [Patrick Kavanagh] 130; 'The Blackbird of Derrycairn' [Austin Clarke] 131; 'The Fool' [Patrick Pearse] 132; 'A Prayer for My Daughter' [W.B. Yeats] 133; 'The Spanish Lady' [Joseph Campbell] 135; 'The Old Road Home' [Teresa Brayton] 137; 'The Lost Ones' [Francis Ledwidge] 137; 'My Mother' [Francis Ledwidge] 138

III From Leinster to Connacht 139

'A Drover' [Padraic Colum] 142; 'Old Woman of the Roads' [Padraic Colum] 143; 'The King of Ireland's Son' [Nora Hopper] 144; 'A Day in Ireland' [Anon., tr. Michael Cavanagh] 145; 'Carrowmore' [AE] 146; 'The County of Mayo [Thomas Lavelle, tr. George Fox] 147; 'Galway Races' [Anon.] 148; 'A Vision of Connacht in the Thirteenth Century'

[James Clarence Mangan] 149; 'Ringleted Youth of My Love' [Anon., tr. Douglas Hyde] 151; 'In a Foreign Land' [Douglas Hyde] 152; 'The Isle of the Blest' [Gerald Griffin] 153; 'O, Sweet Adare' [Gerald Griffin] 154; 'Orange and Green' [Gerald Griffin] 155; 'Pattern of Saint Brendan' [Francis MacManus] 160; 'The Homeward Bound' [Thomas D'Arcy McGee] 161; 'I Think if I Lay Dying' [Winifred Letts] 163; 'Excerpts from an Irish Sequence' [Francis MacManus] 163; 'Ascent of the Reek' [Francis MacManus] 167; 'The Oak of Kildare' [Francis MacManus] 169; 'St John's Tower, Limerick' [Francis MacManus] 170; 'All Over the World' [C.J. Boland] 171

IV From Connacht to Munster 173

'The Blacksmith of Limerick' [Robert Dwyer Joyce] 173; 'The Night We Rode with Sarsfield' [Denis A. McCarthy] 176; 'Drunken Thady' [Michael Hogan] 177; 'Johnny in Killaloe' [Jerome Flood] 189; 'The Limerick Rake' [Anon.] 190; 'The Lambs on the Green Hills' 192; 'For a Bride You have Come!' [Padraic Colum] 193; 'The Bold Fenian Men' [Michael Scanlan] 195; 'Kincora' [tr. James Clarence Mangan] 196; 'Gougaune Barra' [J.J. Callanan] 198; 'The Convict of Clonmel' [tr. J.J. Callanan] 200; 'The Outlaw of Loch Lene' [tr. J.J. Callanan] 201; 'The Three Old Brothers' [Frank O'Connor] 203; 'The Groves of Blarney' [Richard Alfred Milliken] 204; 'Castle Hyde' [Barrett the Weaver] 206; 'Aghadoe' [John Todhunter] 209

V And Back to Tyrrellspass 210

'The Deck beside the Road' [Anon.] 211; 'The Circus Is Coming to Town' [Denis A. McCarthy] 216; 'At Ardaloo' [P. Connor] 219; 'The Blackbird' [Anon.] 221; 'An Ode in Praise of the City of Mullingar' [Anon.] 221; 'The Battle of Tyrrellspass' [Arthur Gerald Geoghegan] 223

Acknowledgments 229

KIELY'S WAY
AROUND
IRELAND

Muckish
Mt Errigal
DONEGAL
Strabane
L.Derg   Drumquin
L.Erne

DERRY
Derry   ANTRIM
Sperrin Mts
Omagh   Belfast
TYRONE   L.Neagh
Dromore   Ballinderry
Armagh
ARMAGH
MONAGHAN
Inniskeen   LOUTH
L.   Oldbridge
Gowna   River
Slane   Boyne   Drogheda
GRANARD   Bellewstown Hill
LONGFORD   Mullingar   Laracor
WESTMEATH   MEATH
Tyrrellspass   Dublin
OFFALY
Birr
WICKLOW
Avondale
R. SHANNON
Killaloe
Limerick
Bruff   TIPPERARY
LIMERICK   Clonmel   WEXFORD
Wexford
Waterford
KERRY   WATERFORD
CORK
Aghadoe   Blarney
Gougane Barra   Cork
Bandon
Kinsale

Collooney
Carrowmore
MAYO   SLIGO
Croagh Patrick
GALWAY
Galway
Ballybritt
L.Derg

Preface

Sometime towards the end of the 1920s, when I was eight or nine, my elder brother, who was a great man for hoarding books, considered that I was mature and literate enough to be allowed access to his collection of *Our Boys*: back numbers of that famed periodical that had been printed and published even before my time. My recollection is that it was indeed a very superior effort, and the feature that most attracted me was a serial called 'Tyrrell of Tyrrellspass'. Perhaps it was simply the fine sound of the names that first got to me, the repetition, the sibilants, which evoked the slapping of scabbards and the creaking of saddle-leather. But I read and reread that blessed serial until I practically knew it by heart and thus became, at an early age, an undoubted authority on the history of the wars of Elizabeth and Hugh O'Neill.

My learning I carried with me – with, I hope, modesty and dignity – to the farmhouse of my Aunt Kate Gormley at Claramore, near Drumquin, a great house for local people coming and going. And, at the age of ten or thereabouts, I most generously decided to give those uninstructed rural people an insight into the history of their country. But one neighbouring farmer, a man called Paddy McCillion (he had a drooping moustache and a dozen or so lovely sons and daughters), elected to play the cynic and pretend that Richard Tyrrell of Tyrrellspass, Hugh O'Neill's famed guerrilla captain, had never existed.

What followed was my first major controversy, and I can still clearly recall the length and intensity of the argument, as I brought up all my learned references from the *Our Boys* to flatten that imperturbable unbeliever. And I can recall, too, the frustration with which I would withdraw from the warm farm-kitchen to the cool privacy of the orchard and there stamp my feet in frenzy. But in the end, generous Paddy confessed to the hoax; we became firm friends and I admitted that he was, after all, a proper Irishman.

So the name of Tyrrellspass has a Proustian effect on me, and when I hear it I see first of all not that handsome little town on the road from Dublin to Galway, but the farm-house at Claramore and the steep hill called Con's Brae, from the top of which you could see, very far away, Mounts Errigal and Muckish. And I see the two deep lakes of Claramore like the eyes of a giant buried in the bogland. And I see Drumard Hill, which had the most fruitful hazel-woods, and out on the heather the bilberries or blayberries or fraughans or what-you-will. And I see the byres and barns and stables, and the two cart-horses, Jumbo and Tom, and the multitude of collie-dogs, and the hearthfire, and the wide flagged floor of the kitchen. And Paddy McCillion's moustache. And I hear the chirping of the crickets.

And, now that I think of it, some time ago I heard a man on the radio say that the cricket, like the corncrake, is now about extinct in Ireland – two of the species disposed of by modern methods and modern living.

Because of that *Our Boys* serial, Richard Tyrrell, captain of cavalry, rides on in my imagination as he once rode in reality for Hugh O'Neill, and with Domhnall Cam O'Sullivan Beare on that final, marathon march from the far end of the Eyeries peninsula to O'Rourke's Leitrim: all to fade away in the end, like so many more out of that time, and die in distant Spain, unchronicled, unchaunted.

But not quite. For always to reawaken my memory there was Geoghegan's 108-line ballad of 'The Battle of Tyrrellspass', in which Tyrrell and O'Connor Offaly, with four hundred men, defeated, it was said, one thousand of the English and their Irish supporters. Here's a bit of the old ballad:

> The baron bold of Trimbleston hath gone, in proud array,
> To drive afar from fair Westmeath the Irish kerns away.
> And there is mounting brisk of steeds and donning shirts of mail,
> And spurring hard to Mullingar 'mong riders of the Pale. [...]
>
> For trooping in rode Nettervilles and Daltons not a few,
> And thick as reeds pranced Nugent's spears, a fierce and godless crew;
> And Nagle's pennon flutters fair, and, pricking o'er the plain,
> Dashed Tuite of Sonna's mailclad men, and Dillon's from Glenshane. [...]
>
> MacGeoghegan's flag is on the hills! O'Reilly's up at Fore!
> And all the chiefs have flown to arms from Allen to Donore,
> And as I rode by Granard moat right plainly might I see
> O'Ferall's clans were sweeping down from distant Annalee.

Now there by the Lord were rolling, resounding lines and a fine iron clangour of Norman names. If you know anything about the ballad history of Ireland you will know that those two verses come from a ballad by Arthur Gerald Geoghegan, whom in old books you will find described simply as the author of 'The Monks of Kilcrea', a book-length series of stories in verse with songs and interludes.

Tyrrell of Tyrrellspass defied Elizabeth's captain, the great Mountjoy, who proclaimed the Norman-Irishman's head for two thousand crowns. But in his midland stronghold, 'seated in a plain, on an island, encompassed with bogs and deep ditches, running in line with the River Brosna, and with thick woods surrounding', Tyrrell laughed at armies and broke them as they came, and when he had to retreat did so successfully, leaving behind him only some wine, corn, cows and garron, and beasts of burden.

He was true to his country, faithful to his friends and a holy terror to the Elizabethan foe – in a skirmish in the O'Moore country he had almost taken the life of Lord Deputy Mountjoy. With his assistance, O'Donnell had evaded Mountjoy's blockade and crossed the Slieve Phelim mountains into Munster. Tyrrell controlled the vanguard after the disaster of Kinsale, he helped MacGeoghegan to defend Dunboy and, in the end of all, fell back to Cavan, his head still on his shoulders. And from Cavan to Spain …

I first encountered this ballad in the two volumes of Edward Hayes's splendid anthology *The Ballads of Ireland* (A. Fullarton & Co., London 1855), loaned to me when I was here at school in Omagh, by that great teacher, M.J. Curry, who also once suggested to me that you could make a book about Ireland by just wandering around, and here, there and everywhere reciting a poem or singing a ballad. I would begin here in the Strule Valley and go here and there until in the end I came to Granard Moat and the countryside that had inspired Geoghegan's resounding ballad. It would be a long and intricate journey and I would meet many songs, poems and ballads on the way.

Then I had the pleasure and privilege of encountering a young Dublin publisher, Antony Farrell of The Lilliput Press, who also thought it was a good idea. For one thing he is an O'Farrell, even if he went to school as far away as Harrow. And he came from the land around Granard Moat, and is very proud of that. So we set together to make a book. And here is how I begin the journey.

I
Ulster

So there, or here, am I, in Sweet Omagh Town, at the beginning of my road of poems and ballads round Ireland. And it occurs to me now that the idea may have been put into my head by the men who taught me when I had the privilege of going to school on Mount St Columba. And not just by M.J. Curry. The teachers came from everywhere and you saw Ireland, and other places, through their eyes and memories and conversations.

Brother Hamill from Belfast had been as far away as China, spoke Chinese, and could talk most eloquently about the multitudinous peoples and great rivers of that vast land. His brother in the world was Mickey Hamill, the famous centre-half, whom I once met.

One Brother Burke came from Dublin and was a rugby football man. The other Brother Burke, a hurling man, hailed from Birdhill, Tipperary, from where you have the heavenly vision of Lough Derg and the stately Shannon spreading, as Spenser said, like a sea.

Brother Clarke, a quiet man, was from Wexford, and he was as proud of it as any rebel-pikeman.

One of my happiest memories is of walking with Brother Walker, long after I had left school, and talking about James Joyce – about whom Brother Rice was a learned authority. Indeed, the first reasonable statement I ever heard about Joyce came from Brother Rice in the middle of a class in trigonometry. Mr Joyce would have been impressed, and grateful.

Anthony Shannon came from Derry, and his memories of student days in Dublin were vivid. The great M.J. Curry was a Clareman, but had been to university in England and could talk most eloquently on all authors, from Cicero to Bret Harte. Frank McLaughlin came from Cork and Leo Sullivan from Wexford, but both of them, one a classicist, the other a scientist, were totally devoted to the Tyrone countryside. And there were others. In the pulpit in the Sacred Heart Church was Dr John McShane, who had studied in Rome and talked in friendship with Gabriele D'Annunzio.

There was Father Lagan who was related to a famous family in the town, and Dr Gallagher, and Father MacBride and Father McGilligan. And in Killyclogher there was Father Paul McKenna, who could quote Robert Burns forever and who brought me one day to Mountfield to visit the aged priestess Alice Milligan.

Patrick Kavanagh in 'The Great Hunger' made a reference to Mullagharn as the hub of a cartwheel of mountains. As I remember, it was something Brother Rice said that set a group of us, one day early in the year, to conquer that mountain. We were Joe Gilroy, Gerry McCanny, Michael Mossy, Larry Loughran, and myself.

Then away with us, up the Killyclogher Burn to Glenhordial, then up and up to the mountain top. Snow still lay in some of the hollows of the mountainside. And when we stood up there together, and looked down on O'Neill's country, and shouted and sang in Irish and English, we felt that we owned Ireland and the world. Perhaps at that moment we did.

That was a day that stays forever in my memory.

We begin the journey, then, if you will bear my company, in my home town of Omagh. Right in the heart of the town the Owenreagh, or Drumragh as we locals call it, accepts the silver Camowen and from that confluence, and north as far as Newtown-Stewart, the bright water is called the Strule. The great lauded names along the splendid river valley between Bessy Bell mountain and the odd-shaped hill of Mary Gray (and Mullagharn and the Gortin hills, out-riders of the Sperrins) were Mountjoy and Blessington. And away back about the time of Bonaparte it is possible that the felling of trees in the Strule Valley helped to pay for the cavortings of Lord and Lady Blessington and the ineffable Count D'Orsay. In time of war there was a demand for timber.

After Waterloo that demand diminished and some of the hired woodcutters were forced to go west over the ocean to make a livelihood, most of them strong young men from the Sperrin Mountains. The local historian, the remarkable Robert Crawford, has described how, on a market-day, those woodsmen would walk the streets of Omagh with great axes on their shoulders and fearing no man. About 1821 this threnody was written for the passing of the woodsmen, Blessington's Rangers – no author have I ever heard named.

THE GREEN FLOWERY BANKS

Thrice happy and blessed were the days of my childhood,
And happy the hours we wandered from school
By old Mountjoy's forest, our dear native wildwood,
On the green flowery banks of the serpentine Strule.

No more will we see the gay silver trout playing,
Or the herd of wild deer through the forest be straying,
Or the nymph and gay swain on the flowery bank straying,
Or hear the loud guns of the sportsmen of Strule.

It is down then by Derry our dear boys are sailing,
Their passions with frantics they scarcely could rule.
Their tongues and their speeches were suddenly failing
While floods of salt tears swelled the waters of Strule.

No more will the fair one of each shady bower
Hail her dear boy of that once happy hour,
Or present him again with a garland of flowers
That they oftimes selected and wove by the Strule.

Their names on the trees of the rising plantation,
Their memories we'll cherish and affection ne'er cool,
For where are the heroes of high or low station
That could be compared with the brave boys of Strule.

But this fatal ship to her cold bosom folds them,
Wherever she goes our fond hearts shall adore them,
Our prayers and good wishes shall still be before them
That their names be recorded and sung to the Strule.

Here's to Patrick McKenna, that renowned bold hero,
His courage proud Derry in vain tried to cool.
There's Wilkinson and Nugent to crown him with glory
With laurels of woodbine they wove by the Strule.

But now those brave heroes are passed all their dangers,
On America's shores they won't be long strangers,
And they'll send back their love to famed Blessington's Rangers,
Their comrades and friends and the fair maids of Strule.

In the part of Omagh town where I grew up there was born, and lived for a while, a man by the name of Francis Carlin. He wrote some poems, then went off to the USA, where that hard world was not overkind to him. He was contacted, or unearthed, in New York City by the poet Padraic Colum and his wife, Mary, who found him a job in Macy's department store: an odd place, perhaps, for a poet who, downriver from Omagh at Douglas Bridge, had seen a vision of the last of the Rapparees. Carlin died in 1945.

THE BALLAD OF DOUGLAS BRIDGE

By Douglas Bridge I met a man
Who lived adjacent to Strabane,
Before the English hung him high
For riding with O'Hanlon.

The eyes of him were just as fresh
As when they burned within the flesh;
And his boot-legs were wide apart
From riding with O'Hanlon.

'God save you, Sir,' I said with fear,
'You seem to be a stranger here.'
'Not I,' said he, 'nor any man
Who rode with Count O'Hanlon.'

'I know each glen from North Tyrone
To Monaghan. I have been known
By every clan and parish since
I rode with Count O'Hanlon.'

'Before that time,' said he to me,
'My fathers owned the land you see;
But now they're out among the moors
A-riding with O'Hanlon.'

'Before that time,' said he with pride,
'My fathers rode where now they ride
As Rapparees, before the time
Of trouble and O'Hanlon.'

'Good night to you, and God be with
The tellers of the tale and myth,
For they are of the spirit-stiff
That rode with Count O'Hanlon.'

'Good night to you,' said I, 'and God
Be with the chargers, fairy-shod,
That bear the Ulster heroes forth
To ride with Count O'Hanlon.'

By Douglas Bridge we parted, but
The Gap o' Dreams is never shut,
To one whose saddled soul to-night
Rides out with Count O'Hanlon.

A great friend in my home town was Captain William Maddin Scott, head of a notable family and, as owner of Scott's Mills, a good and fair employer. Captain Scott had prepared an anthology, *A Hundred Years A-Milling,* relating his family to the town and the Tyrone countryside, which they had honoured and aided for so long by their presence. When Seán MacRéamoinn and myself featured the book on a Radio Éireann programme called (how hopefully!) 'The Nine Counties of Ulster', the Captain was mightily pleased and I was elevated to being a dinner-guest at the Scott mansion at Lisnamallard, where I was introduced to the Rev. Marshall of Sixmilecross.

Marshall was a most gracious and learned gentleman, and a prime authority on Ulster folk-dialect. When the Captain told me that 'our friend Marshall' was 'a Doctor of Divinity' we both laughed merrily. Now there was no reason why Marshall of Sixmilecross should not be a Doctor of Divinity, or a doctor of anything and everything; what set us laughing was that the learned doctor had also written in his *Tyrone Ballads* (The Quota Press, Belfast 1951) of the sad plight of the man in Drumlister:

ME AN' ME DA

I'm livin' in Drumlister,
An' I'm gettin' very oul'
I have to wear an Indian bag
To save me from the coul'.
The deil a man in this townlan'
Wos claner raired nor me,
But I'm livin' in Drumlister
In clabber to the knee.

Me da lived up in Carmin,
An' kep' a sarvint boy;
His second wife was very sharp,
He birried her with joy:

Now she was thin, her name was Flynn,
She come from Cullentra,
An' if me shirt's a clatty shirt
The man to blame's me da.

Consarnin' weemin' sure it was
A constant word of his,
'Keep far away from them that's thin,
Their temper's aisy riz.'
Well, I knew two I thought wud do,
But still I had me fears,
So I kiffled back and forrit
Between the two, for years.

Wee Margit had no fortune
But two rosy cheeks wud plaze;
The farm of lan' wos Bridget's,
But she tuk the pock disayse:
An' Margit she wos very wee,
An' Bridget she was stout,
But her face wos like a gaol dure
With the bowlts pulled out.

I'll tell no lie on Margit,
She thought the worl' of me;
I'll tell the truth, me heart wud lep
The sight of her to see.
But I was slow, ye surely know,
The raison of it now,
If I left her home from Carmin
Me da wud rise a row.

So I swithered back an' forrit
Till Margit got a man;
A fella come from Mullaslin
An' left me jist the wan.
I mind the day she went away,
I hid one strucken hour,
An' cursed the wasp from Cullentra
That made me da so sour.

But cryin' cures no trouble,
To Bridget I went back,
An' faced her for it that night week
Beside her own thurf-stack.
I axed her there, an' spoke her fair,
The handy wife she'd make me.
I talked about the lan' that joined
– Begob, she wudn't take me!

So I'm livin' in Drumlister,
An' I'm gettin' very oul'.
I creep to Carmin wanst a month
To thry an' make me sowl:
The deil a man in this townlan'
Wos claner raired nor me,
An' I'm dyin' in Drumlister
In clabber to the knee.

From that same time in the past dates a friendship with a
priest, Father Paul McKenna, who brought me one day to
the old rectory in the village of Mountfield, where the aged
poet Alice Milligan then lived in a dusty grandeur recalling
the home of Miss Haversham in *Great Expectations*. But the
garden where she played in her girlhood could still be seen
at the end of Omagh town where one road divides to make
three: at a place called the Swinging Bars, where there once
may have been a toll-gate.

WHEN I WAS A LITTLE GIRL

When I was a little girl,
In a garden playing,
A thing was often said
To chide us, delaying:

When after sunny hours,
At twilight's falling,
Down through the garden's walks
Came our old nurse calling –

Ulster

'Come in! for it's growing late,
And the grass will wet ye!
Come in! or when it's dark
The Fenians will get ye.'

Then, at this dreadful news,
All helter-skelter,
The panic-struck little flock
Ran home for shelter.

And round the nursery fire
Sat still to listen,
Fifty bare toes on the hearth,
Ten eyes a-glisten.

To hear of a night in March,
And loyal folk waiting,
To see a great army of men
Come devastating –

An Army of Papists grim,
With a green flag o'er them,
Red-coats and black police
Flying before them.

But God (who our nurse declared
Guards British dominions)
Sent down a fall of snow
And scattered the Fenians.

'But somewhere they're lurking yet,
Maybe they're near us,'
Four little hearts pit-a-pat
Thought 'Can they hear us?'

Then the wind-shaken pane
Sounded like drumming;
'Oh!' they cried, 'tuck us in,
The Fenians are coming!'

Four little pairs of hands
In the cots where she led those,
Over their frightened heads
Pulled up the bedclothes.

But one little rebel there,
Watching all with laughter,
Thought 'When the Fenians come
I'll rise and go after.'

Wished she had been a boy
And a good deal older –
Able to walk for miles
With a gun on her shoulder.

Able to lift aloft
The Green Flag o'er them
(Red-coats and black police
Flying before them);

And, as she dropped asleep,
Was wondering whether
God, if they prayed to Him,
Would give fine weather.

There was a time when, without offence and in mixed (sectarian, not sexual) company, it was possible to sing 'The Sash My Father Wore'. This may no longer be advisable. But the magic flute may, because of its very intractability, retain a heavenly neutrality. Scholars and flautists will know that there are variant renderings.

THE OULD ORANGE FLUTE

In the County Tyrone, near the town of Dungannon,
Where many's the ruction myself had a han' in,
Bob Williamson lived, a weaver by trade,
And we all of us thought him a stout Orange blade.
On the Twelfth of July, as it yearly did come,
Bob played on the flute to the sound of the drum:
You may talk of your harp, the piano or lute,
But there's none could compare with the ould Orange flute.

But this sinful deceiver he took us all in
And married a Papish called Brigid McGinn,
Turned Papish himself and forsook the ould cause
That gave us our freedom, religion and laws.

Now the boys of the place made some comment upon it,
And Bob had to fly to the province of Connacht:
He flew with his wife and his fixtures to boot,
And along with the rest went the ould Orange flute.

At the chapel on Sundays to atone for his past deeds
He said Paters and Aves on his knees and his brown beads,
And after a while at the priest's own desire
He took the ould flute for to play in the choir.
He took the ould flute for to play at the Mass,
But the instrument shivered and sighed 'Oh Alas!'
And blow as he would, though he made a great noise,
The flute would play only the Protestant Boys.

Bob flustered and fingered and got in a splutter
And dipped the ould flute in the blessed holy water.
He thought that the dipping would bring a new sound,
When he blew it again it played Croppies Lie Down.
He could whistle his utmost and finger and blow
To play Papish tunes, but the flute wouldn't go.
Kick the Pope, the Boyne Water and Croppies Lie Down,
And no Papish squeak in it all could be found.

At the Council of priests that was held the next day
'Twas decided to banish the ould flute away.
Since they couldn't knock heresy out of its head,
They bought Bob a new one to play in its stead.
So the ould flute was doomed and its fate was pathetic,
'Twas sentenced and burned at the stake as heretic.
As the flames roared around it they heard a strange noise,
The ould flute was still playing the Protestant Boys.

My mother came from the village of Drumquin and
numbered among her friends Felix Kearney, who wrote
poems, some of them meant to be sung. I had the honour of
meeting him in his old age, and in the presence of the man
himself I heard Paddy Tunney sing Kearney's song about
'The Hills above Drumquin'.

And as I Rode by Granard Moat

God bless the Hills of Donegal,
I've heard their praises sung,
In days long gone beyond recall
When I was very young.
Then I would pray to see a day
Before Life's course be run
When I could sing the praises
Of the Hills above Drumquin.

I love the Hills of Dooish,
Be they heather clad or lea,
The wooded glens of Cooel
And the Fort on Dun-na-ree.
The green clad slopes of Kirlish
When they meet the setting sun
Descending in its glory on the
Hills above Drumquin.

Drumquin, you're not a city
But you're all the world to me.
Your lot I will not pity
Should you never greater be.
For I love you as I knew you
When from school I used to run
On my homeward journey through you
To the Hills above Drumquin.

I have seen the Scottish Highlands,
They have beauties wild and grand,
I have journeyed in the Lowlands
'Tis a cold and cheerless land.
But I always toiled content
For when each hard day's work was done
My heart went back at sunset
To the Hills above Drumquin.

When the whins across Drumbarley
Make the fields a yellow blaze;
When the heather turns to purple
On my native Dressog braes;
When the sandstone rocks of Claramore
Are glistening in the sun,

16

Then Nature's at her grandest
On the hills above Drumquin.

This world is sad and dreary,
And the tasks of life are sore.
My feet are growing weary
I may never wander more.
For I want to rest in Langfield
When the sands of life are run
In the sheltering shade of Dooish
And the Hills above Drumquin.

But it was in the village of Dromore, County Tyrone, that I
first heard the poem in praise of 'Drumquin Creamery'.
How many creameries in Ireland, or in the wide world,
have been so honoured?

You farmers and traders of Ireland
I pray will you listen with ease,
For they say it's as true as the Gospel.
So listen, kind friends, if you please.

Till I tell you about a new creamery
That only was opened last June,
For the good of the parish of Langfield,
While some of them left it full soon.

For the good of the parish of Langfield,
For no other cause was it built,
To help the poor struggling farmers
With which Langfield it once had been filled.

CHORUS
So here's to our own local creamery,
And to the wide world be it known,
Drumquin it has got the best creamery,
The best in the County Tyrone.

We have got an excellent committee
That meets upon each Monday night.
Two or three of our members
Most generally end in a fight.

And as I Rode by Granard Moat

For the one won't give in to the other,
And, maybe, we haven't some fun
Away down by the parish of Langfield
In our creamery down at Drumquin.

We have got an excellent committee,
Religion it makes, there's no doubt.
For we have got JPs and clergy,
And some of them Orangemen stout.
We have two or three 'Ninety-Eight men,
Beneath the same banner they stand,
To represent that same banner
The banner of God Save the Land.

We have got an excellent committee
That lies in close to the town,
Charlie Hall, Tommy Law and Joe Dolan,
Pat Morris and Charlie McKeown.

John Corry that sweeps the Cornmarket,
Jamey Corry from Bomacatall,
Pat the Tip from behind Dooish Mountain,
John Futhy from no place at all.

We have got an excellent reporter,
You all know him well, Quentin Todd,
He reports all affairs to the papers.
That's something that seems very odd.

For Quentin himself, he's no writer,
But not one single word could you speak,
But he'd lift and take straight down to Omagh,
To the *Tyrone Constitution* next week.

So, you farmers and traders of Ireland,
I hope you'll take care and be wise.
Try and keep up your creamery
Till you see how your parish will rise.

It'll be one of the finest in Ulster,
It'll be one of the best ever seen.
It'll be one of the finest in Ireland,
Our creamery down at Drumquin.

And if you feel up to it you may sing all that to the tune to which the Aghalee heroes marched to the banks of the Boyne.

The Man from God Knows Where

The man from that odd place did not originate in the North of Ireland, nor did the woman who wrote the poem about him come from my own neighbourhood; but for me personally, this piece belongs to Omagh and to its town hall. For at some time in the 1930s Brother Hamill decided that, stupid as I was – as he often told me – I might yet be able to learn off by heart (or head) and recite in public from the town-hall stage the entire poem about Thomas Russell, the United Irishman, the Man from God Knows Where. This elocutionary feat was to be performed during a concert otherwise given over to celebrities from all arts and parts, but mostly from Derry city. Derry people, we were always told, were very musical.

Brother Hamill, besides being brother-in-the-flesh to Mickey Hamill, one of the greatest-ever centre-halves, and himself had been away out there trying to pressurize the Chinese into Christianity, or into soccer-football, or something. So when he told me that I would step out there and recite, little choice had I.

Shivering in the wings I stood, as a doctor from Derry sang in a fine soprano about the merry, merry pipes of Pan. To this day that song frightens me. I hated Pan, whoever he was. For I knew that as soon as the lovely lady was finished, I was doomed to be pushed forward to recite. Which, with the help of God and Brother Hamill, I did:

> Into our townlan', on a night of snow,
> Rode a man from God-knows-where;
> None of us bade him stay or go,
> Nor deemed him friend, nor damned him foe.

But we stabled his big roan mare;
For in our townlan' we're a decent folk,
And if he didn't speak, why none of us spoke,
And we sat till the fire burned low.

We're a civil sort in our wee place,
So we made the circle wide
Round Andy Lemon's cheerful blaze,
And wished the man his length of days
And a good end to his ride.
He smiled in under his slouchy hat –
Says he: 'There's a bit of a joke in that,
For we both ride different ways.'

The whiles we smoked we watched him stare
From his seat fornenst the glow.
I nudged Joe Moore: 'You wouldn't dare
To ask him, who he's for meeting there,
And how far he has got to go.'
And Joe wouldn't dare, nor Wully Scott,
And he took no drink – neither cold nor hot –
This man from God-knows-where.

It was closin' time, an' late forbye,
When us ones braved the air –
I never saw worse (may I live or die)
Than the sleet that night, an' I says, says I:
'You'll find he's for stopping there.'
But at screek o' day, through the gable pane,
I watched him spur in the peltin' rain,
And I juked from his rovin' eye.

Two winters more, then the Trouble Year,
When the best that man can feel
Was the pike he kapt in hidin' near,
Till the blood o' hate and the blood o' fear
Would be redder nor rust on the steel.
Us ones quiet from mindin' the farms,
Let them take what we gave wi' the weight o' our arms,
From Saintfield to Kilkeel.

Ulster

In the time o' the Hurry, we had no lead —
We all of us fought with the rest —
And if e'er a one shook like a tremblin' reed,
None of us gave neither hint nor heed.
Nor ever even'd we'd guessed.
We men of the North had a word to say,
An' we said it then, in our own dour way,
An' we spoke as we thought was best.
All Ulster over, the weemen cried
For the stan'in' crops on the lan' —
Many's the sweetheart an' many's the bride
Would liefer ha' gone till where He died,
And ha' mourned her lone by her man.
But us ones weathered the thick of it,
And we used to dander along and sit,
In Andy's, side by side.

What with discourse goin' to and fro,
The night would be wearin' thin,
Yet never so late when we rose to go
But someone would say: 'Do ye min' thon snow,
An' the man who came wanderin' in?'
And we be to fall to the talk again,
If by any chance he was One o' Them —
The man who went like the Win'.

Well 'twas gettin' on past the heat o' the year
When I rode to Newtown Fair;
I sold as I could (the dealers were near —
Only three pounds eight for the Innish steer,
An' nothin' at all for the mare!)
I met M'Kee in the throng o' the street,
Says he: 'The grass has grown under our feet
Since they hanged young Warwick here.'

And he told me that Boney had promised help
To a man in Dublin town.
Says he: 'If you've laid the pike on the shelf,
Ye'd better go home hot-fut by yourself,
An' once more take it down.'
So by Comber road I trotted the grey

And never cut corn until Killyleagh
Stood plain on the risin' groun'.

For a wheen o' days we sat waitin' the word
To rise and go at it like men.
But no French ships sailed into Cloughey Bay,
And we heard the black news on a harvest day
That the cause was lost again;
And Joey and me, and Wully Boy Scott,
We agreed to ourselves we'd as lief as not
Ha' been found in the thick o' the slain.

By Downpatrick Gaol I was bound to fare
On a day I'll remember, feth,
For when I came to the prison square
The people were waitin' in hundreds there,
An' you wouldn't hear stir nor breath!
For the sodgers were standing, grim an' tall,
Round a scaffold built there fornenst the wall,
An' a man stepped out for death!

I was brave an' near to the edge of the throng,
Yet I knowed the face again.
An' I knowed the set, an' I knowed the walk
An' the sound of his strange up-country talk,
For he spoke out right an' plain.
Then he bowed his head to the swinging rope,
Whiles I said, 'Please God' to his dying hope,
And 'Amen' to his dying prayer,
That the Wrong would cease and the Right prevail
For the man that they hanged at Downpatrick gaol
Was the Man from GOD-KNOWS-WHERE!

[Florence M. Wilson]

For people who talk familiarly about the Loughshore there is only one lough in Ireland or anywhere else. Those who have the pleasure of living by Lough Erne will mention the name of the lough, but the hardy people who live by Lough

Neagh assume that there is One Supreme Lough and that everybody should know as much. The man who wrote about 'Old Ardboe' had no doubts on the matter:

> Farewell my native green-clad hills,
> Farewell my shamrock plains,
> Ye verdant banks of sweet Lough Neagh,
> Ye silvery winding streams.
> Though far from home in green Tyrone
> The flora oft I praise
> That adorns you Killyclopy
> Where I spent my boyhood days.
>
> Shall I ever see those valleys
> Where in boyhood days I roved,
> Or wander in those June green woods
> With friends I dearly loved?
> Shall I no more by Lough Neagh's shore
> E'er pass the summer day,
> Or hear again the lark's sweet strain
> Or the blackbird's blithesome lay?
>
> Shall I ever stray by the Washingbay
> The wary trout to coy,
> Or set my line on an evening fine
> By the shores of green Mountjoy?
> Will my oars ne'er rest on the wild wave crest,
> Will I see the salmon play
> While sailing o'er from Tyrone's green shore
> Bount for Antrim's placid bay?
>
> Shall I e'er behold Shane's castle bold
> Or look upon Massarene,
> Will my cot ne'er land on the banks of the Bann,
> Coney Island or Roskeen.
> Will the autumn gale e'er fill my sail
> Or the dim declining moon,
> See me tempest-tossed on the shores of Doss
> Or the raging bay of Toome.

And as I Rode by Granard Moat

Shall I ever rove by Belmont's Grove
Or Carnan's lofty hill,
Or hear again the fairy tale
Of the rath behind the hill?
Will the nightingale that charms the vale
By me be heard no more,
As I watch at eve the wild drake leave
For the bog of Sweet Dromore?

See where yon ancient structure lies,
Beneath the silent shore,
Where people tell saintly monks did dwell
In the penal days of yore,
And now upon the crumbling walls
The climbing ivies grow.
As alone I stray at the close of day
Through the sweet bogs of Ardboe.

My friends they have in America
All the heart of man desires,
Their pockets filled with dollar bills
And dressed in grand attire.
But they'd give it all for one country ball
Beside the old hearth stone,
Of a cottage near Lough Neagh, so dear,
Our own sweet Irish home.

But I hope to gaze on your flowery braes
Ere seven long years come round
And hands to clasp in friendship's grasp
Of those I left behind.
For you Ardboe my tears do flow
When I think and call to mind
My parents dear, my friends sincere,
And my comrades true and kind.

But since, alas! long years may pass
Still I toast that beauteous isle,
That short or long, o'er that land of song
The star of peace may shine,
May plenty bloom from Bann to Toome

And the shamrock verdant grow
Green o'er those graves by Lough Neagh's waves
Near the Cross of old Ardboe.

Ballinderry is in the Land of the Loughshore and is mentioned in more than one poem as a place with a name so musical well deserves to be. Samuel Ferguson's great 'Lament for Thomas Davis' begins at Ballinderry but moves on to embrace all of Ireland and many, many years.

I walked through Ballinderry in the spring-time,
When the bud was on the tree;
And I said, in every fresh-ploughed field beholding
The sowers striding free,
Scattering broadside forth the corn in golden plenty
On the quick seed-clasping soil
'Even such, this day, among the fresh-stirred hearts of Erin,
Thomas Davis, is thy toil!'

I sat by Ballyshannon in the summer,
And saw the salmon leap;
And I said, as I beheld the gallant creatures
Spring glittering from the deep,
Through the spray, and through the prone heaps striving onward
To the calm clear streams above,
'So seekest thou thy native founts of freedom, Thomas Davis,
In thy brightness of strength and love!'

I stood on Derrybawn in the autumn,
And I heard the eagle call,
With a clangorous cry of wrath and lamentation
That filled the wide mountain hall,
O'er the bare deserted place of his plundered eyrie;
And I said as he screamed and soared,
'So callest thou, thou wrathful soaring Thomas Davis,
For a nation's rights restored!'

And alas! to think but now, and thou art lying,
Dear Davis, dead at thy mother's knee;
And I, no mother near, on my own sick-bed,

That face on earth shall never see;
I may lie and try to feel that I am dreaming,
I may lie and try to say, 'Thy will be done' –
But a hundred such as I will never comfort Erin
For the loss of the noble son!

Young husbandman of Erin's fruitful seed-time,
In the fresh track of danger's plough!
Who will walk the heavy toilsome, perilous furrow
Girt with freedom's seed-sheets now?
Who will banish with the wholesome crop of knowledge
The daunting weed and the bitter thorn,
Now that thou thyself art but a seed for hopeful planting
Against the Resurrection morn?
Young salmon of the flood-tide of freedom
That swells around Erin's shore!
Thou wilt leap around their loud oppressive torrent
Of bigotry and hate no more;
Drawn downward by their prone material instinct,
Let them thunder on the rocks and foam –
Thou hast leapt, aspiring soul, to founts beyond their raging
Where troubled waters never come.

But I grieve not, Eagle of the empty eyrie,
That thy wrathful cry is still;
And that the songs alone of peaceful mourners
Are heard to-day on Erin's hill;
Better far, if brothers' war be destined for us
(God avert that horrid day, I pray),
That ere our hands be stained with slaughter fratricidal
Thy warm heart should be cold in clay.

But my trust is strong in God, Who made us brothers,
That He will not suffer their right hands
Which thou hast joined in holier rites than wedlock
To draw opposing brands.
Oh, many a tuneful tongue that thou mad'st vocal
Would lie cold and silent then;
And songless long once more, should often-widowed Erin
Mourn the loss of her brave young men.

Oh, brave young men, my love, my pride, my promise,
'Tis on you my hopes are set,
In manliness, in pride, in justice,
To make Erin a nation yet,
Self-respecting, self-relying, self-advancing,
In union or in severance, free and strong –
And if God grant this, then, under God, to Thomas Davis
Let the greater praise belong.

From Ballinderry to Baile-liosan is only a jump or a short flight over the water, or a run around the roads. When you get there you are in the world of that great poet Joseph Campbell, the Mountainy Singer:

'TIS PRETTY TAE BE IN BAILE-LIOSAN

'Tis pretty tae be in Baile-liosan,
'Tis pretty tae be in green Magh-luan;
'Tis prettier tae be in Newtownbreda,
Beeking under the eaves in June.
The cummers are out wi' their knitting and spinning,
The thrush sings frae his crib on the wa',
And o'er the white road the clachan caddies
Play at their marlies and goaling-ba'.

O, fair are the fields o' Baile-liosan,
And fair are the faes o' green Magh-luan;
But fairer the flowers of Newtownbreda,
Wet wi' dew in the eves o' June.
'Tis pleasant tae saunter the clachan thoro'
When day sinks mellow o'er Dubhais Hill,
And feel their fragrance sae softly breathing
Frae croft and causey and window-sill.

O, brave are the haughs o' Baile-liosan,
And brave are the halds o' green Magh-luan;
But braver the hames o' Newtownbreda,
Twined about wi' the pinks o' June.
And just as the face is sae kindly withouten,
The heart within is as guid as gold –

Wi' new fair ballants and merry music,
And cracks cam' down frae the days of old.

'Tis pretty tae be in Baile-liosan,
'Tis pretty tae be in green Magh-luan;
'Tis prettier tae be in Newtownbreda,
Beeking under the eaves in June.
The cummers are out wi' their knitting and spinning,
The thrush sings frae his crib on the wa',
And o'er the white road the clachan caddies
Play at their marlies and goaling-ba'.

We are travelling too fast; we must pay a decorous farewell
to my native town and to another lough which lies close to
it. Nobody quite knows who wrote this first poem or song.

SWEET OMAGH TOWN

Ah! from proud Dungannon to Ballyshannon
And from Cullyhanna to Old Ardboe
I've roused and rambled, caroused and gambled
Where songs did thunder and whiskey flow.
It's light and airy I've tramped through Derry
And to Portaferry in the County Down
But with all my raking and undertaking
My heart was aching for sweet Omagh Town.

When life grew weary, aye, and I grew dreary
I set sail for England from Derry Quay
And when I landed, sure 'twas fate commanded
That I to London should make my way
Where many a gay night from dark to daylight
I spent with people of high renown
But with all their splendour and heaps to spend sure
My heart was empty for sweet Omagh Town.

Then further going my wild oats sowing
To New York City I crossed the sea
Where congregations of rich relations
Stood on the harbour to welcome me
In grand apparel like Duke or Earl

They tried to raise me with sword and crown
But with all their glamour and uproarious manner
My lips would stammer – sweet Omagh Town.

And when life is over and I shall hover
Above the gates where Saint Peter stands
And he shall call me for to install me
Among the saints in those golden lands
And I shall answer 'I'm sure 'tis grand sir
For to play the harp and to wear the crown
But I, being humble, sure I'll never grumble
If Heaven's as charming as sweet Omagh Town.'

That other lough, small and unpretentious, a couple of miles from the town is called, modestly, Lough Muck. But the name is not, by any means, intended to lower it to the level of a mudbath. It was fine to swim in, and the best place in the world in which to catch perch. The original name was, needless to say, Loch na Muice, the Lake of the Pig, that mythological pig which, slumbering on the enchanted ocean, misled the Milesians.

Lough Muck lay slumbering there, like the monstrous pig, but doing no harm to anybody. A relative of mine, however, considered calmly that it brought enchantment to all who looked on it. He was a man called Frank McCrory, a Shavian, a Wellsian, and a man of music who could play everything from the 'cello to the ocarina. In his youth (about 1919) he had even been a famous footballer. He wrote songs for the neighbourhood and he worked up this fantasy about two boys from the town who had been drinking a bit, wandered off and were bemused by the enchanted lake ...

THE TREACHEROUS WAVES OF LOUGHMUCK

Me and Andy one ev'nin were strollin'
As the sun was beginning to set
And when just outside Drumragh new graveyard

And as I Rode by Granard Moat

A young Loughmuck sailor we met.
He brought us along to his liner
That was breasting the waves like a duck
And that's how we started our ill-fated cruise
On the treacherous waves of Loughmuck.
(Repeat last two lines for chorus)

As our ship glided over the water
We all gazed at the landscape we knew
First we passed Clanabogan's big lighthouse
Then the Pigeon Top came into view.
But alas as we sped o'er those waters
Soon we all were with horror dumbstruck
For without any warning a big storm arose
On the treacherous waves of Loughmuck.

The storm came on with thunder and lightning
And the big waves lashed mountains high
Our ship was tossed hither and thither
Then black darkness came over the sky.
The passengers shrieked out in terror
As our ship Aughadulla rock struck,
Me and Andy was all that was saved from the wreck
On the treacherous waves of Loughmuck.

People talk of the great Loch Ness monster
And to see it they come young and old
But the monsters we saw that wild evenin'
Leave the Loch Ness boy out in the cold.
Sharks, sea-lions, whales, alligators
With mouths that could swallow a truck
Oh the sights that we saw as we waited for death
On the treacherous waves of Loughmuck.

There we were like two Robinson Crusoes
Miles away from Fireagh Orange Hall
Though we starved on that rock for a fortnight
Not a ship ever came within call.
At last we decided to swim it
Though we don't like to brag of our pluck
After swimmin' for two days we reached Creevan Bay
On the treacherous waves of Loughmuck.

There we lay on that beach quite exhausted
Till a man with a big dog drew near
He shouted out, 'Hi, clear away out of that.
'Faith I want no drunk Omey boys here!'
He said we'd been drinkin' and sleepin'
Since the clock in his parlour four struck
And that was the end of our ill-fated cruise
On the treacherous waves of Loughmuck.

It has just occurred to me that I may have taken on an impossible task: to move round Ireland to the ultimate goal of Tyrrellspass, and to move in an orderly way, remembering and reciting as I go. That thought comes as I struggle with the following odd and informative verses, presented to me about thirty years ago when I was writing a newspaper column. I had mentioned the love that Mayo people have for their own placenames, as in the song:

Ballina, Ballinrobe, Baal and Bohola,
Newport, and Foxford a few miles below.
Then on to Inishteague and down to Manulla,
You'll always find true friends in the County Mayo ...

And I wondered if, in that respect, Mayo people surpassed those of any other Irish county. A friend of mine, a Dublinman, suggested that I set up an inter-county competition in place-name balladry and have broadcast, to encourage the competitors, Father James B. Dollard's 'Song of the Little Villages'. Here are some of the verses:

The pleasant little villages that grace the Irish Glyns,
Down among the wheat-fields, up among the whins,
The little white-walled villages crowding close together,
Clinging to the old sod in spite of wind and weather:
Ballytarsney, Ballymore, Ballyboden, Boyle,
Ballingarry, Ballymagorry by the banks of Foyle,
Ballylaneen, Ballyporeen, Bansha, Ballisodare,
Ballybrack, Ballinalack, Barna, Ballyclare.

And as I Rode by Granard Moat

The cosy little villages that shelter from the mist
Where the great Western Walls by ocean spray are kissed.
The happy little villages that cuddle in the sun
When blackberries ripen and the harvest work is done.
Corrymeela, Croaghnakeela, Clogher, Cahirciveen,
Cappagharne, Carrigaloe, Cashel and Coosheen,
Castlefin and Carrigtwohill, Crumlin, Clara, Clane,
Carrigaholt, Carrigaline, Cloughjordan and Coolrain.

The dreamy little villages where, by the fire at night,
Old Shanachies, with ghostly tales, the boldest hearts affright.
The crooning of the wind-blast in the wailing banshee's cry,
And when the silver hazels stir they say the fairies sigh.
Kilfenora, Kilfinane, Kinnitty, Killylea,
Kilmoganny, Kiltimagh, Kilronan and Kilrea,
Killeshandra, Kilmacow, Killiney, Kilashee,
Killenaule, Kilmyshall, Killorglin and Killeagh.

Leave the little villages, over the black seas go,
Learn the stranger's welcome, learn the exile's woe.
Leave the little villages but think not to forget,
Afar they'll rise before your eyes to rack your bosoms yet.
Moneymore, Moneygall and Moyne,
Mullinahone, Mullinavat, Mullagh and Mooncoin,
Shanagolden, Shanballymore, Stranorlar and Slane,
Toberheena, Toomeyvara, Tempo and Strabane.

On the Southern Llanos-north, where strange light gleams,
Many a yearning exile sees them in his dreams.
Dying voices murmur, past all pain and care:
'Lo! the little villages, God has heard our prayer.'
Lisdoonvarna, Lisadell, Lisdargan, Lisnaskea,
Portglenone, Portarlington. Portumna, Portmagee,
Clonegall and Clonegowan, Cloondara and Clonae,
God bless the little villages and guard them night and day.

There's more. But even the most eloquent and energetic elocutionist might rest content with that much for his party-piece – a portion of an alphabet of Ireland – and so might his audience.

I can close my eyes and hear, in my garrison home town, the pipes of the British Army playing long lines of unfortunate soldiers to the railway station on their way to Europe in 1940. The tune went with William Allingham's 'The Winding Banks of Erne'. How many of those fellows had ever heard of or seen Belashanny? How many of them ever came back?

Adieu to Belashanny! where I was bred and born;
Go where I may I'll think of you, as sure as night and morn;
The kindly spot, the friendly town, where every one is known,
And not a face in all the place but partly seems my own;
There's not a house or window, there's not a field or hill,
But east or west, in foreign lands, I'll recollect them still;
I leave my warm heart with you, though my back I'm forced to turn –
So adieu to Belashanny and the winding banks of Erne!

No more on pleasant evenings we'll saunter down the Mall,
When the trout is rising to the fly, the salmon to the fall.
The boat comes straining on her net, and heavily she creeps,
Cast off, cast off – she feels the oars, and to her berth she sweeps;
Now fore and aft keep hauling and gathering up the clew,
Till a silver wave of salmon rolls in among the crew.
Then they may sit with pipes alit, and many a joke and yarn. –
Adieu to Belashanny and the winding banks of Erne!

The music of the waterfall, the mirror of the tide,
When all the green-hilled harbour is full from side to side,
From Portnasun to Bulliebawns, and round the Abbey Bay,
From rocky Inis Saimer to Coolnargit sandhills grey;
While far upon the southern line, to guard it like a wall,
The Leitrim mountains, clothed in blue, gaze calmly over all,
And watch the ship sail up or down, the red flag at her stern; –
Adieu to these, adieu to all the winding banks of Erne!

Farewell to you, Kildoney lads, and all that pull an oar,
A lugsail set, or haul a net, from the Point to Mullaghmore;
From Killybegs to bold Slieve League, that ocean-mountain steep,
Six hundred yards in air aloft, six hundred in the deep;
From Dooran to the Fairy Bridge, and round by Tullen strand,

And as I Rode by Granard Moat

Level and long, and white with waves, where gull and curlew stand;
Head out to sea, when on your lee the breakers you discern! –
Adieu to all the billowy coast and winding banks of Erne!

Farewell, Coolmore – Bundoran! and your summer crowds that run
From inland to see with joy th'Atlantic-setting sun;
To breathe the buoyant salted air, and sport among the waves;
To gather shells on sandy beach, and tempt the gloomy caves;
To watch the flowing, ebbing tide, the boats, the crabs, the fish;
Young men and maids to meet and smile, and form a tender wish;
The sick and old in search of health, for all things have their turn –
And I must quit my native shore and the winding banks of Erne!

Farewell to every white cascade from the Harbour to Belleek,
And every pool where fins may rest, and ivy-shaded creek;
The sloping fields, the lofty rocks, where ash and holly grow,
The one split yew-tree gazing on the curving flood below;
The Lough that winds through islands under Turaw mountain green;
And Castle Caldwell's stretching woods, with tranquil bays between;
And Breesie Hill, and many a pond among the heath and fern; –
For I must say adieu – adieu to the winding banks of Erne!

The thrush will call through Camlin groves the live-long summer day;
The waters run by mossy cliff, and banks with wild flowers gay;
The girls will bring their work and sing beneath a twisted thorn,
Or stray with sweethearts down the path among the growing corn;
Along the riverside they go, where I have often been –
O never shall I see again the happy days I've seen!
A thousand chances are to one I never will return –
Adieu to Belashanny and the winding banks of Erne!

Adieu to evening dances, when merry neighbours meet,
And the fiddle says to boys and girls, 'Get up and shake your feet!'
To seanachas and wise old talk of Erin's days gone by –
Who trenched the rath on such a hill, and where the bones may lie
Of saint or king or warrior chief; with tales of fairy power,
And tender ditties sweetly sung to pass the twilight hour.
The mournful song of exile is now for me to learn –
Adieu, my dear companions on the winding banks of Erne!

Now measure from the Commons down to each end of the Port,
Round the Abbey, Moy and Knather – I wish no one any hurt;
The Main Street, Back Street, College Lane, the Mall and Portnasun,
If any foes of mine are there, I pardon every one.
I hope that man and womankind will do the same by me;
For my heart is sore and heavy at voyaging the sea.
My loving friends I'll bear in mind, and often fondly turn
To think of Belashanny and the winding banks of Erne.

If ever I'm a moneyed man, I mean, please God, to cast
My golden anchor in the place where youthful years were passed;
Tho' heads that now are black and brown must meanwhile gather grey
New faces rise by every hearth and old ones drop away –
Yet dearer still that Irish hill than all the world beside;
It's home, sweet home, where'er I roam, through lands and waters wide.
And if the Lord allows me, I surely will return
To my native Belashanny and the winding banks of Erne.

Long ago, when I listened with the utmost reverence to
William Butler Yeats reading his poetry out loud on the
radio, I was young enough almost to think that I could
make a better job of it myself. The odd thing is that over the
years his voice still echoes most memorably. But never did I
hear him read the strange poem that follows.

There is no record, as far as I know, that the great poet
himself ever did the arduous Lough Derg pilgrimage, but he
did defend the tradition of pilgrimage against the remarkable
Rev. Cesar Otway, who saw it all as degraded superstition.
Reason, it seems, was in the early nineteenth century trying
to creep into Ireland. Yeats, as a young man, thought that
Otway showed little respect for an ancient custom that had
been hallowed by the verse of Calderon and the feet of
centuries of pilgrims. However, it was Otway who, in an
odd way, gave a first chance to a young writer by the name
of William Carleton. And Carleton's story 'The Lough Derg
Pilgrim' found its echoes in the Yeats poem.

And as I Rode by Granard Moat

I fasted for some forty days on bread and buttermilk,
For passing round the bottle with girls in rags or silk,
In country shawl or Paris cloak, had put my wits astray,
And what's the good of women, for all that they can say
Is fol de rol de rolly O.

Round Lough Derg's holy island I went upon the stones,
I prayed at all the Stations upon my marrow-bones,
And there I found an old man, and though I prayed all day
And that old man beside me, nothing would he say
But fol de rol de rolly O.

All know that all the dead in the world about that place are stuck,
And that should mother seek her son she'd have but little luck
Because the fires of Purgatory have ate their shapes away;
I swear to God I questioned them, and all they had to say
Was fol de rol de rolly O.

A great black ragged bird appeared when I was in the boat;
Some twenty feet from tip to tip had it stretched rightly out,
With flopping and with flapping it made a great display,
But I never stopped to question, what could the boatman say
But fol de rol de rolly O.

Now I am in the public-house and lean upon the wall,
So come in rags or come in silk, in cloak or country shawl,
And come with learned lovers or with what men you may,
For I can put the whole lot down and all I have to say
Is fol de rol de rolly O.

Yet another great poet had the unusual good fortune to
encounter the ghost of William Carleton – a very solid
ghost, for Carleton was a strong, solid man. Carleton and
Seamus Heaney met somewhere around the enchanted
Knockmany Hill, in the Clogher Valley, about which
Carleton himself wrote one of his few poems. From any
high ground in that neighbourhood you may see the glisten
of the magical waters of Lough Erne.

Ulster

Cloud lifted off the mountain. Thin sunlight
moved a pale green over the hill-farms.
Lough Erne came clear, bog-cotton dried out white.

I was parked on a high moor, listening
to peewits and wind blowing round the car,
when something came to life in the driving mirror,

a man walking fast, in an overcoat
and boots, bareheaded, big, determined
in his sure haste along the crown of the road

like a farmer bearing down on trespassers.
There was no house for miles, I had not passed him
nor anyone, nor seen a sign of campers,

and I somehow felt myself the challenged one.
The car door slammed. I was suddenly out
standing face to face with William Carleton

who once in Georgian Ireland listened for
the gun-butt to come cracking on the door
the night the night-self of his Orange neighbour

swooped to hammer home the shape of things.
'On this road you caught up with the two women,'
I said, faking confidence. 'Your Lough Derg Pilgrim

haunts me every time I cross this mountain –
as if I am being followed or following.
I'm on my way there now to do the station.'

'O holy Jesus Christ, does nothing change?'
His head jerked sharply side to side and up
like a diver's surfacing after a plunge,

then with a look that said, let this cup
pass, he seemed to take cognizance again
of where he was: the road, the mountain top,

and the air, benign after the soft rain,
worked on his anger visibly, until:
'It is a road you travel on your own.

I who read *Gil Blas* in the reek of flax
and smelt the bodies rotting on their gibbets
and saw their looped slime gleaming from the sacks –

hard-mouthed Ribbonmen and Orange bigots
made me into the old fork-tongued turncoat
who mucked the byre of our politics.

If times were hard, then I could be hard too.
I made the smiler in me sink the knife.
And maybe there's a lesson there for you

whoever you are, wherever you came out of,
for though there's something natural in your smile
there's something in it strikes me as defensive.'

'I have no mettle for the angry role,'
I said. 'I come from County Derry,
born in earshot of an Hibernian hall

where a band of Ribbonmen played hymns to Mary.
By then that brotherhood was a frail procession
staggering back home drunk on Patrick's Day

in collarettes and sashes fringed with green.
Obedient strains like theirs tuned me first
and not that harp of unforgiving iron

the Fenians strung. A lot of what you wrote
I heard and did: this Lough Derg station,
flax-pullings, dances, summer cross-roads chat

and the shaky local voice of education.
All that. And always, Orange drums.
And neighbours on the roads at night with guns.'

'I know, I know, I know, I know,' he said,
'nothing changes. But make sense of what comes,
remember everything and keep your head.'

'Green slime that we called glit, wet mushrooms,
dark-clumped grass where cows or horses dunged,
the cluck when pith-lined chestnut-shells split open

in your hand, the melt of shells corrupting,
I seem to have known all these things forever.'
I felt my hand being shaken now by Carleton:

'All this is like a trout kept in a spring
or maggots sown in wounds for desperate ointment –
another life that cleans our element.'

No poet of our time speaks with greater authority and feeling about that corner of Ireland than John Montague. He spent his boyhood and early youth between there and Armagh city, with occasional visits to Sweet Omagh Town.

LIKE DOLMENS ROUND MY CHILDHOOD,
THE OLD PEOPLE

Like dolmens round my childhood, the old people.
Jamie MacCrystal sang to himself,
A broken song without tune, without words;
He tipped me a penny every pension day,
Fed kindly crusts to winter birds.
When he died, his cottage was robbed,
Mattress and money-box torn and searched.
Only the corpse they didn't disturb.

Maggie Owens was surrounded by animals,
A mongrel bitch and shivering pups,
Even in her bedroom a she-goat cried.
She was a well of gossip defiled,
Fanged chronicler of a whole countryside;
Reputed a witch, all I could find
Was her lonely need to deride.

The Nialls lived along a mountain lane
Where heather bells bloomed, clumps of foxglove.
All were blind, with Blind Pension and Wireless,
Dead eyes serpent-flicked as one entered
To shelter from a downpour of mountain rain.

And as I Rode by Granard Moat

Crickets chirped under the rocking hearthstone
Until the muddy sun shone out again.

Mary Moore lived in a crumbling gatehouse,
Famous as Pisa for its leaning gable.
Bag-apron and boots, she tramped the fields
Driving lean cattle from a miry stable.
A by-word for fierceness, she fell asleep
Over love stories, Red Star and Red Circle,
Dreamed of gypsy love rites, by firelight sealed.

Wild Billy Eagleson married a Catholic servant girl
When all his Loyal family passed on:
We danced round him shouting 'To Hell with King Billy',
And dodged from the arc of his flailing blackthorn.
Forsaken by both creeds, he showed little concern
Until the Orange drums banged past in the summer
And bowler and sash aggressively shone.

Curate and doctor trudged to attend them,
Through knee-deep snow, through summer heat,
From main road to lane to broken path,
Gulping the mountain air with painful breath.
Sometimes they were found by neighbours,
Silent keepers of a smokeless hearth,
Suddenly cast in the mould of death.

Ancient Ireland, indeed! I was reared by her bedside,
The rune and the chant, evil eye and averted head,
Fomorian fierceness of family and local feud.
Gaunt figures of fear and of friendliness,
For years they trespassed on my dreams,
Until once, in a standing circle of stones,
I felt their shadows pass
Into that dark permanence of ancient forms.

A LOST TRADITION

All around, shards of a lost tradition:
From the Rough Field I went to school
In the Glen of the Hazels. Close by
Was the bishopric of the Golden Stone;
The cairn of Carleton's homesick poem.

Scattered over the hills, tribal
And placenames, uncultivated pearls.
No rock or ruin, dun or dolmen
But showed memory defying cruelty
Through an image-encrusted name.

The heathery gap where the Rapparee,
Shane Barnagh, saw his brother die –
On a summer's day the dying sun
Stained its colours to crimson:
So breaks the heart, Brish-mo-Cree.

The whole landscape a manuscript
We had lost the skill to read,
A part of our past disinherited;
But fumbled, like a blind man,
Along the fingertips of instinct.

The last Gaelic speaker in the parish,
When I stammered my school Irish
One Sunday after mass, crinkled
A rusty litany of praise:
Tá an Ghaeilge againn arís ... *

Tír Eoghain: Land of Owen,
Province of the O'Niall;
The ghostly tread of O'Hagan's
Barefoot gallowglasses marching
To merge forces in Dun Geanainn

Push southward to Kinsale!
Loudly the war-cry is swallowed
In swirls of black rain and fog
As Ulster's pride, Elizabeth's foemen,
Founder in a Munster bog.

Paddy Tunney, poet, singer and story-teller, although he
now lives near Letterkenny, is very much a man of Erne.
For he was born and grew up and learned his music in the
enchanted land where the Stone Fiddle of Castlecauldwell
still stands in memory of the fiddler drowned in the lough.

*We have the Irish again.

In his book, *The Stone Fiddle,* you will find the words and music of this song, which Paddy introduces under the title, 'Gael Meets Gael':

In the whole corpus of traditional song couched in the borrowed Béarla, there is none to compare with the high-minded effusions of our hedge-school-master poets. These songs are readily recognizable by the plen-itude of classical allusion they contain and by the adaptation of the Gaelic assonantal rhyme, used extensively by the Gaelic Aisling poets of the eighteenth century.

When the classes dispersed and the master roamed, with the great god Pan down in the reeds by the river, then surely it was that his mind took fire and he wrote such a song as 'Lough Erne Shore'.

One morning as I went a fowling, bright Phoebus adorned the plain,
'Twas down by the shores of Lough Erne, I met with this wonderful dame,
Her voice was so sweet and so pleasing, these beautiful notes she did sing,
The innocent fowl of the forest their love unto her they did bring.

It being the first time I saw her, my heart it did lep with surprise
I thought that she could be no mortal, but an angel who fell from the skies,
Her hair it resembled gold tresses, her skin was as white as the snow,
And her cheeks were as red as the roses that bloom around Lough Erne Shore.

When I found that my love was eloping, these words unto her I did say,
O take me to your habitation, for Cupid has led me astray.
For ever I'll keep the commandments, they say that it is the best plan,
Fair maids who do yield to mens' pleasure, the Scripture does say they are wrong.

O Mary don't accuse me of weakness, for treachery I do disown,
I'll make you a lady of honour, if with me this night you'll come home.
O had I the lamp of Great Aladdin, his rings and his genie, that's more,
I would part with them all for to gain you and live upon Lough Erne Shore.

'The Maid of Lough Gowna Shore'

I find this on an ancient broadsheet presented to me many years ago by that great bibliophile and man of letters, M.J. MacManus:

One morning as I went a fowling,
As Phoebus adorned the plain,
'Twas down by the shades of Lough Gowna,
I met with this lovely young dame.
Her voice was so sweet and so charming,
These beautiful notes she did sing,
The innocent fowls of the forest
My love unto her they did bring.

It being the first time I had seen her,
My heart she had fill'd with surprise,
I thought that she could be no mortal,
But an angel that fell from the skies.
Her hair it resembled gold laces,
Her skin was as white as the snow,
Her cheeks were as red as the roses
That blow upon Lough Gowna's shore.

I found that my love was eloping,
And this unto her I did say,
Come, bring me to your habitation,
For Cupid has led me astray.
My parents they left me some riches,
Five thousand I have now in store,
And I'll spend it with you, my dear darling,
In pleasure upon Lough Gowna shore.

Kind sir, I don't believe in such notions,
I know that you are not sincere,
Although you have done your endeavours
To leave my poor heart in a snare
For ever I'll keep the commandment,
I'm told that it is the best plan,
For the maid that will yield to man's pleasure
The Scripture does say she is wrong.

And as I Rode by Granard Moat

Dear Mary, do not accuse me of weakness,
For treachery I do disown,
I'll make you a lady of honour,
If with me this night you'll come home.
For had I the treasures of England,
The East and West Indies, that's more,
I'd part with it all for to gain you,
And live upon Lough Gowna shore.

Kind sir, I am but a poor female,
For riches indeed I have none,
Besides, we are not one persuasion,
My heart lies in the Church of Rome
Then you would fulfil your desires,
Like Numbers in the days of yore,
And you'd leave me bewailing misfortune
Through grief on Lough Gowna shore.

O, Mary, if you were persuaded,
In wedlock we'd join our hands,
For believe me it was not my notion
To force you to break the commands.
So tell me your mind in a moment,
For you are the one I adore,
My heart it is lodged in your bosom,
This night near Lough Gowna shore.

Now my theme of this female is ended,
A blessing she'll gain from above,
A fortune she gain'd with her darling,
And that by enchantments of love.
I wish I was able to praise her,
Her equal I ne'er saw before,
So Mary got married to Thomas,
And he brought her from Lough Gowna shore.

Margaret Barry of the travelling people used to wander this
country and London and portions of the USA with Michael
Gorman, one of the famous men of music from around

Templehouse lake in south Sligo. Michael had learned to play the fiddle at the building of a house near Mucklety Mountain for people by the name of Devaney, relations of my own. Michael was a boy at the time and working at the building was Jamesie Gannon, then a famous fiddler. Jamesie undertook the teaching of Michael, even to the writing of the music on ceiling boards, which were afterwards built into the house. 'Music built the towers of Troy,' the poet said.

Here is one of Margaret's favourite songs, which so often she sang in the old Brazen Head in Dublin.

THE MANTLE SO GREEN

As I went out a walking one morning in June,
To view the fields and the meadows in full bloom,
I espied a young damsel, she appeared like a queen,
With her costly fine robes and her mantle so green.

I stood with amazement and was struck with surprise,
I thought her an angel that fell from the skies.
Her eyes were like diamonds, her cheeks like the rose,
She is one of the fairest that nature composed.

I said, my pretty fair maid, if you will come with me,
We'll both join in wedlock, and married we'll be,
I'll dress in rich attire, you'll appear like a queen,
With costly fine robes and your mantle so green.

She answered, young man, you must me excuse,
For I'll wed with no man, you must be refused,
To the woods I'll wander to shun all men's view,
For the lad that I love is in famed Waterloo.

If you won't marry tell me your love's name,
For I being in battle I might know the same.
Draw near to my garment and there will be seen,
His name all embroidered on my mantle of green.

In raising her mantle there I did behold
His name and surname were in letters of gold,
Young William O'Reilly appeared to my view,
He was my chief comrade in famed Waterloo.

We fought so victorious where bullets did fly,
In the field of honour your true love does lie,
We fought for three days till the fourth afternoon,
He received his death-summons on the eighteenth of June.

But when he was dying I heard his last cry,
If you were here, lovely Nancy, contented I'd die,
Peace is proclaimed, and the truth I declare,
Here is your love token, the gold ring I wear.

She stood in amazement, the paler she grew,
She flew to my arms with a heart full of woe,
To the woods I'll wander for the lad I adore.
Rise up, lovely Nancy, your grief I'll remove,

Oh, Nancy, dearest Nancy, 'tis I won your heart,
In your father's garden that day we did part ...

At this point the broadsheet breaks off abruptly, leaving the voice of the singer, literally, on and in the air.

Padraic Colum used frequently to lament that the custom or style of speaking verse had gone from the world, or from the part of the world we lived in. He was saying what he thought to be the truth, although thirty years ago I did hear and see a man standing, dizzily and high, on a barstool in the old White Horse, on Burgh Quay in Dublin, to tell the intellectual assembly that on the slopes of Killiecrankie all that night our soldiers lay. Such sights and sounds, though, are very rare nowadays, and if I once did know a Dublin lawyer who could speak, well and word-perfect, all the verses of George Meredith's 'Love in a Valley', it must be admitted that he was a most unusual man.

There are schools of elocution, and verse-speaking

groups and societies, but that's not the same thing as standing up in a room, or a snug, and speaking out spontaneously the verse that is in you. Readings by poets of their own poetry have become quite fashionable, which is a good thing – if what is fashionable is ever good – and proves that people are interested in hearing poetry read out loud. It is to be hoped that when we read poetry we do so out loud even if nobody is listening bar the walls or the wind.

Padraic Colum spoke his own verse in a low, emphasized sing-song diction that may have originated with the celebrated *Sixth Reader*. It was undemonstrative but effective. My father used the same voice when I learned from him that a chieftain to the Highlands bound cried, 'Boatman, do not tarry'. Or that our bugles sang truce, for the night-clouds had lowered and the sentinel stars set their watch in the sky. Or that around the fire one winter's night the farmer's rosy children sat. These poems I had never read or seen in print until recently, but they stayed in the memory more or less accurately for many years.

You might not find your favourite piece for recitation within the covers of this book. If not I beg your forgiveness; in my wanderings here and there I might have missed it. Maybe the decent people were chanting it in some townland that I bypassed. But I assume that every man and woman must already know their own favourite recitation off by heart and thus are not dependent on myself or anyone else to provide them with the words. The maker of any anthology should be entitled, within reason, to meet criticism halfway by saying simply: 'Consider, please, what is in this book. Not what is not in it.' Or, if you want your own anthology, make it yourself. And the maker of a book of songs and recitations should further be allowed to say: 'Before you carp or criticize, do me the favour of learning off by heart every poem that is in this book.'

Memorizing maketh a full man. The man who knows, say, a hundred and one poems off by heart should never be short of a party piece, and if, by mischance, he should ever find himself in solitary confinement, he will have a faithful and enduring companion.

I may seem deliberately capricious in the order and arrangement of the poems, songs and recitations; but there is, I hope, a certain method in that. You do not, or should not, recite by categories, and I will not so arrange this book. Nor by authors: it pleases me and may have pleased them that Oscar Wilde should stand side by side with Felix Kearney, the ballad-maker from Clanabogan Planting. There is a higher democracy in the speaking of poems.

Nor should one recite by themes. For to different people the same poem may have different themes, and I would like this book to be used just as the possessors of it would recite on the inspiration or impulse of the moment; they would learn the poems as they come on them, and change the mood as they please. Nobody would wish to stand all the time mouthing patriotism or stuttering love. You will more easily memorize what you fancy at the moment.

Yet it may be wise at times to compel and concentrate the memory, so I will cut or diminish no poem: this would be to insult both poets and reciters. To present things entire may be a good extension for all our memories, particularly those of the young, who seem to rest content, like the rooks in the trees, with a few rhythmic sounds endlessly repeated.

What a splendid test for memory, diction and histrionic ability is that great heroic poem, the lament for Nell Flaherty's beautiful drake, who, like Patrick Kavanagh's gods, made his own importance. Percy French sang his praises and mourned his passing.

Ulster

NELL FLAHERTY'S DRAKE

My name it is Nell, quite candid I tell
And I live near Cootehill, I'll never deny.
I had a large drake, the truth for to spake,
That my grandmother left me and she going to die.
He was wholesome and sound and weighed twenty pound,
The universe round I would rove for his sake.
Bad luck to the robber, be him drunk or sober,
That murdered Nell Flaherty's beautiful drake.

His neck it was green – then most rare to be seen –
He was fit for a queen of the highest degree;
His body so white that it would you delight,
He was plump, fat and heavy and brisk as a bee;
The dear little fellow, his legs they were yellow,
He'd fly like a swallow and swim like a hake;
But some wicked savage, to grease his white cabbage,
Has murder'd Nell Flaherty's beautiful drake.

May his pig never grunt, may his dog never hunt,
That a ghost may him haunt in the dark of the night;
May his hen never lay, may his ass never bray,
And his goat fly away like an ould paper kite.
May his cat and her fleas the wretch ever tease,
And the pinching north breeze make him tremble and shake;
May a thirsty pup drink up the last sup
Of the monster that murdered Nell Flaherty's drake.

May his pipe never smoke, may his taypot be broke,
And, to add to the joke, may his kettle not boil;
May he twist in his bed till the moment he's dead,
May he often be fed on paraffin oil.
May he swell with the gout, may his grinders fall out,
May he roar, bawl and shout with a horrid toothache,
May his temples wear horns, and all his toes corns –
The monster that murder'd Nell Flaherty's drake.

May his spade never dig, may his sow never pig,
May no one with wit with him ever deal,
May his door have no latch, may his home have no thatch,
May his turkey not hatch, may the rats eat his meal;

May every old fairy from Cork to Dunleary
Dip him till weary in cowld pond or lake,
Where the pike and the eel will lance the heel
Of the monster that murder'd Nell Flaherty's drake.

May his dog yelp and growl with both hunger and cowld,
May his wife always scowld till his brain goes astray,
May the curse of each hag that e'er carried a bag
Light on the vag, till his beard turns to grey;
May monkeys still bite him, and gorillas affright him,
And everyone slight him, asleep and awake,
May weasels still gnaw him, and jackdaws still claw him –
The monster that murder'd Nell Flaherty's drake.

The only good news I have to diffuse
Is that long Peter Hughes and blind piper Craik
And big Bob Manson and buck-tooth'd Hanson:
Each man has a grandson of my beautiful drake;
My bird has dozens of nephews and cousins,
And one I must get, or my heart it will break.
To keep my mind aisy – or else I'll run crazy.
This ends the whole song of Nell Flaherty's drake.

Here is James Clarence Mangan interpreting, with some help, what the tribal bard had to say about the passing of the Maguire of Fermanagh:

O'HUSSEY'S ODE TO THE MAGUIRE

Where is my Chief, my master, this bleak night, mavrone!
O, cold, cold, miserably cold is this bleak night for Hugh,
Its showery, arrowy, speary sleet pierceth one through and through,
Pierceth one to the very bone!

Rolls real thunder? Or was that red livid light
Only a meteor? I scarce know; but through the midnight dim
The pitiless ice-wind streams. Except the hate that persecutes him
Nothing hath crueller venomy might.

Ulster

An awful, a tremendous night is this, meseems!
The flood-gates of the rivers of heaven, I think, have been burst wide –
Down from the overcharged clouds, like unto headlong ocean's tide,
Descends grey rain in roaring streams.

Though he were even a wolf ranging the round green woods,
Though he were even a pleasant salmon in the unchainable sea,
Though he were a wild mountain eagle, he could scarce bear, he,
This sharp, sore sleet, these howling floods.

O, mournful is my soul this night for Hugh Maguire!
Darkly, as in a dream, he strays! Before him and behind
Triumphs the tyrannous anger of the wounding wind,
The wounding wind, that burns as fire!

It is my bitter grief – it cuts me to the heart –
That in the county of Clan Darry this should be his fate!
O, woe is me, where is he? Wandering, houseless, desolate,
Alone, without or guide or chart!

Medreams I see just now his face, the strawberry-bright,
Uplifted to the blackened heavens, while the tempestuous winds
Blow fiercely over and around him, and the smiting sleet-shower blinds
The hero of Galang tonight!

Large, large affliction unto me and mine it is,
That one of his majestic bearing, his fair, stately form,
Should thus be tortured and o'erborne – that this unsparing storm
Should wreak its wrath on head like his!

That his great hand, so oft the avenger of the oppressed,
Should this chill, churlish night, perchance, be paralysed by frost –
While through some icicle-hung thicket – as one lorn and lost –
He wails and wanders without rest.

The tempest-driven torrent deluges the mead,
It overflows the low banks of the rivulets and ponds –
The lawns and pasture-grounds lie locked in icy bonds
So that the cattle cannot feed.

The pale bright margins of the streams are seen by none.
Rushes and sweeps along the untameable flood on every side –
It penetrates and fills the cottagers' dwellings far and wide –
Water and land are blent in one.

Through some dark woods, 'mid bones of monsters, Hugh now strays,
As he confronts the storm with anguished heart, but manly brow –
O! what a sword-wound to that tender heart of his were now
A backward glance at peaceful days.

But other thoughts are his – thoughts that can still inspire
With joy and an onward-bounding hope the bosom of Mac Nee –
Thoughts of his warriors charging like bright billows of the sea,
Borne on the wind's wings, flashing fire!

And though frost glaze to-night the clear dew of his eyes,
And white ice-gauntlets glove his noble fine fair fingers o'er,
A warm dress is to him that lightning-garb he ever wore,
The lightning of the soul, not skies.

Hugh marched forth to the fight – I grieved to see him so depart;
And lo! to-night he wanders frozen rain-drenched, sad, betrayed –
But the memory of the lime-white mansions his right hand hath laid
In ashes warms the hero's heart!

Once upon a time, thirty years ago, I found myself writing a
serial radio-script on the 'Songs of Young Ireland' – for
which the music was performed by the Radio Éireann
Singers. The previous series, featuring 'Moore's Melodies'
and scripted by Brinsley MacNamara, lasted for a very long
time, and he was often teased by the novelist Philip Rooney
about writing the songs himself and attributing them to
Thomas Moore, so as to keep the programme going.

I was more or less challenged to make the songs of
Young Ireland last longer than the songs of the Sweet
Melodist. As it happened, I failed. But I consulted the then
Greatest Living Authority on the matter, Colm Ó Lochlainn
at The Sign of the Three Candles, and he told me that I
could bring the songs of Young Ireland as close to myself as
Francis A. Fahey, who sang of Kinvara and the Ould Plaid
Shawl, and could go back as far as William Drennan writing
about 'The Wake of William Orr':

Ulster

There our murdered brother lies;
Wake him not with woman's cries;
Mourn the way that manhood ought –
Sit in silent trance of thought.

Write his merits on your mind;
Morals pure and manners kind;
In his head, as on a hill,
Virtue placed her citadel.

Why cut off in palmy youth?
Truth he spoke, and acted truth.
'Countrymen, unite,' he cried,
And died for what our Saviour died.

God of peace and God of love!
Let it not Thy vengeance move –
Let it not Thy lightnings draw –
A nation guillotined by law.

Hapless Nation, rent and torn,
Thou wert early taught to mourn;
Warfare for six hundred years!
Epoch marked with blood and tears!

Hunted thro' thy native grounds,
Or flung reward to human hounds,
Each one pulled and tore his share,
Heedless of thy deep despair.

Hapless Nation! hapless Land!
Heap of uncementing sand!
Crumbled by a foreign weight:
And, by worse, domestic hate.

God of mercy! God of peace!
Make this mad confusion cease;
O'er the mental chaos move,
Through it speak the light of love.

Monstrous and unhappy sight!
Brothers' blood will not unite;
Holy oil and holy water
Mix, and fill the world with slaughter.

Who is she with aspect wild?
The widowed mother with her child –
Child new stirring in the womb
Husband waiting for the tomb!

Angel of this sacred place,
Calm her soul and whisper peace –
Cord, or axe, or guillotine,
Make the sentence – not the sin.

Here we watch our brother's sleep:
Watch with us, but do not weep:
Watch with us thro' dead of night –
But expect the morning light.

To balance one Ulster voice against another, let us hear that great, gracious and highly related lady, Charlotte Elizabeth, singing the Pride of Londonderry on the banks of the Foyle. The politics of what now follows and of Drennan's poem may seem to get a little bit entangled; but the words, even in our time, are worth remembering:

THE MAIDEN CITY

Where Foyle his swelling waters rolls northward to the main,
Here, Queen of Erin's daughters, fair Derry fixed her reign:
A holy temple crowned her, and commerce graced her street,
A rampart wall was round her, the river at her feet;
And here she sate alone, boys, and looking from the hill,
Vowed the maiden on her throne, boys, would be a Maiden still.

From Antrim crossing over, in famous Eighty-Eight,
A plumed and belted lover came to the Ferry Gate:
She summoned to defend her, our sires – a beardless race –
Who shouted No Surrender! and slammed it in his face.
Then, in a quiet tone, boys, they told him 'twas their will
That the maiden on her throne, boys, should be a Maiden still.

Next, crushing all before him, a kingly wooer came
(The royal banner o'er him, blushed crimson deep for shame);
He showed the Pope's commission, nor dreamed to be refused,

She pitied his condition, but begged to stand excused.
In short, the fact is known, boys, she chased him from the hill,
For the maiden on her throne, boys, would be a Maiden still.

On our brave sires descending, 'twas then the tempest broke,
Their peaceful dwellings rending, 'mid blood, and flame, and smoke,
That hallowed grave-yard yonder, swells with the slaughtered dead –
Oh brothers! pause and ponder, it was for us they bled;
And while their gift we own, boys – the fane that tops our hill,
Oh, the maiden on her throne, boys, shall be a Maiden still.

Nor wily tongue shall move us, nor tyrant arm affright,
We'll look to One above us who ne'er forsook the right;
Who will, may crouch and tender the birthright of the free,
But, brothers, no surrender, no compromise for me!
We want no barrier stone, boys, no gates to guard the hill,
Yet the maiden on her throne, boys, shall be a Maiden still.

When in the early 1940s Thomas MacGreevy came back to
Ireland from Paris, where he had been the friend of James
Joyce and T.S. Eliot, *et alibi aliorum sanctorum martyrum et
confessorum,* the first place I had the honour of seeing him
was at a meeting of the English Literature Society of University College, Dublin, when everything, or nearly
everything, happened in Earlsfort Terrace. (Somewhere else
at that time there was, I have heard, a war going on.)

At that meeting of great minds Thomas MacGreevy was
in the chair, I was in the mob. The matter under discussion
was: 'That Shakespeare was a nineteenth-century myth.'
The high moment in the proceedings came when another
member of the mob made a precise, well-calculated speech
describing his own personal relationship with William
Shakespeare, and some of the things they had been up to
together, in all sorts of places from Strabane to Stratford-
upon-Avon. The speaker was Kevin, a brother of Brian

O'Nolan: Kevin, a man of infinite jest, went on to be a Professor of Classics.

We worried for a bit as to how the learned and distinguished chairman might, or might not, accept such flippancy. But he rose to it, recalling how, as a young man in Tarbert, County Kerry, he had once welcomed Shakespeare to that happy place, and led the Bard around the roads of the Kingdom.

In later years I was honoured to become a friend of Thomas MacGreevy. One evening at sunset I stood with him on Capel Street Bridge, and we looked at the light dying on the old, wine-coloured, quayside houses. And he, who had seen so much of splendid Paris, said to me: 'Dublin is very beautiful.' And because I was an Ulsterman, and because he knew I admired it, he recited his poem about Red Hugh O'Donnell:

AODH RUADH Ó DOMHNAILL

Juan de Juni the priest said
Each J becoming H;

Berruguete, he said,
And the G was aspirate;

Ximenez, he said then
And aspirated first and last.

But he never said
And – it seemed odd – he
Never had heard
The spirated name
Of the centuries-dead
Bright-haired young man
Whose grave I sought.

All day I passed
In greatly built gloom
From dusty gilt tomb

Marvellously wrought
To tomb
Rubbing
At mouldy inscriptions
With fingers wetted with spit
And asking
Where I might find it
And failing.

Yet when
Unhurried –
Not as at home
When heroes, hanged, are buried
With non-commissioned officers' bored maledictions
Quickly in the gaol yard –

They brought
His blackening body
Here
To rest
Princes came
Walking behind it

And all Valladolid knew
And out to Simancas all knew
Where they buried Red Hugh.

What follows is in a very different style, but is as much part of Donegal as any memory of Red Hugh.

Many of us have happy memories of Rann-na-Feirsde in the Rosses, and of Coláiste Brighde, and the lovely people in the houses all around, who led us gently into a knowledge of our own language, and of the music and traditions that went with it. My own memories of that enchanted place go back to 1940, getting to know the O'Grianna family and listening to the singing of Hudie Devaney.

Here now, an echo over a half-century, is one of his songs, translated by Paddy Tunney:

THE FORSAKEN SOLDIER

When I rose like a Russian that morning
No cross on my forehead I signed,
For the thought that my true love had left me
It drove me clean out of my mind.
I reached for a scythe that hung high in the hawthorn,
Fell to her with file and a blue sharping-stone,
And stripped to the waist in the cornfield
I cut half the harvest alone.

My feet are too long without leather,
My pockets much longer want gold,
I envy the old mountain weather
For his love tales need never be told.
They say that his heartache all winter will tarry
And lead to the tomb before next Easter day,
And the boys that I hurled with will carry
My corpse to its rest in the clay.

If I were stretched prone with the fever
Or seven years under the ground,
And you came to my tomb, love, and called me
I would rise from the dead with one bound.
My sorrow that death did not strike down my father,
'Fore he drove me to drink & the King's own armie,
In the boneyard my hard bed is waiting,
O my darling have pity on me.

But we are lingering too long in Ulster and yet have touched
on only a few portions of the Noble Nine Counties. Voices
call to me from here and there. Listen now to one from
Inniskeen, in the County Monaghan, telling us about
memories of 'A Christmas Childhood'.

I

One side of the potato-pits was white with frost –
How wonderful that was, how wonderful!
And when we put our ears to the paling-post
The music that came out was magical.

Ulster

The light between the ricks of hay and straw
Was a hole in Heaven's gable. An apple tree
With its December-glinting fruit we saw –
O you, Eve, were the world that tempted me

To eat the knowledge that grew in clay
And death the germ within it! Now and then
I can remember something of the gay
Garden that was childhood's. Again

The tracks of cattle to a drinking-place,
A green stone lying sideways in a ditch
Or any common sight, the transfigured face
Of a beauty that the world did not touch.

II

My father played the melodeon
Outside at our gate;
There were stars at the morning east
And they danced to his music.

Across the wild bogs his melodeon called
To Lennons and Callans.
As I pulled on my trousers in a hurry
I knew some strange thing had happened.

Outside the cow-house my mother
Made the music of milking;
The light of her stable-lamp was a star
And the frost of Bethlehem made it twinkle.

A water-hen screeched in the bog,
Mass-going feet
Crunched the wafer-ice on the pot-holes,
Somebody wistfully twisted the bellows wheel.

My child poet picked out the letters
On the grey stone,
In silver the wonder of a Christmas townland,
The winking glitter of a frosty dawn.

Cassiopeia was over
Cassidy's hanging hill,

I looked and three whin bushes rode across
The horizon – the Three Wise Kings.

An old man passing said:
'Can't he make it talk' –
The melodeon. I hid in the doorway
And tightened the belt of my box-pleated coat.

I nicked six nicks on the door-post
With my penknife's big blade –
There was a little one for cutting tobacco.
And I was six Christmases of age.

My father played the melodeon,
My mother milked the cows,
And I had a prayer like a white rose pinned
On the Virgin Mary's blouse.

Many years ago I remember coming out, much moved,
from a performance of Synge's *Deirdre of the Sorrows* in the
old Abbey Theatre. Siobhán MacKenna had played Deirdre,
and walking home, all the way to the far end of Clontarf, I
could still hear her voice in those great final speeches. This
epic story had absorbed so many of the writers of that time:
Yeats, George Russell, the lot. I was set muttering to myself
the tribute that the poet James Stephens paid the tragic
queen:

DEIRDRE

Do not let any woman read this verse;
It is for men, and after them their sons
And their sons' sons.

The time comes when our hearts sink utterly;
When we remember Deirdre and her tale,
And that her lips are dust.

Once she did tread the earth; men took her hand;
They looked into her eyes and said their say,
And she replied to them.

More than a thousand years it is since she
Was beautiful; she trod the waving grass;
She saw the clouds.

A thousand years! The grass is still the same,
The clouds as lovely as they were that time
When Deirdre was alive.

But there has never been a woman born
Who was so beautiful, not one so beautiful
Of all the women born.

Let all men go apart and mourn together;
No man can ever love her; not a man
Can ever be her lover.

No man can bend before her; no man say –
What could one say to her? There are no words
That one could say to her!

Now she is but a story that is told
Beside the fire! No man can ever be
The friend of that poor queen.

If Deirdre can be placed anywhere in Ireland or in the world
it would be around Armagh, and Eamhain Macha. With the
tragic brothers, and the raving king, and a woman will be
young forever. After all, Cleopatra's other name, or perhaps
one of her other names, was Egypt. Samuel Ferguson heard
Deirdre lamenting in splendid words the passing, and trag-
edy, of the sons of Uisneach:

The lions of the hill are gone,
And I am left alone – alone –
Dig the grave both wide and deep,
For I am sick, and fain would sleep!

The falcons of the wood are flown,
And I am left alone – alone –
Dig the grave both deep and wide,
And let us slumber side by side.

And as I Rode by Granard Moat

The dragons of the rock are sleeping,
Sleep that wakes not for our weeping:
Dig the grave and make it ready;
Lay me on my true Love's body.

Lay their spears and bucklers bright
By the warriors' sides aright;
Many a day the Three before me
On their linked bucklers bore me.

Lay upon the low grave floor,
'Neath each head, the blue claymore;
Many a time the noble Three
Redden'd those blue blades for me.

Lay the collars, as is meet,
Of their greyhounds at their feet;
Many a time for me have they
Brought the tall red deer to bay.

Oh! to hear my true Love singing,
Sweet as sound of trumpets ringing:
Like the sway of ocean swelling
Roll'd his deep voice round our dwelling.

Oh! to hear the echoes pealing
Round our green and fairy sheeling,
When the Three, with soaring chorus,
Pass'd the silent skylark o'er us.

Echo now, sleep, morn and even –
Lark alone enchant the heaven! –
Ardan's lips are scant of breath –
Neesa's tongue is cold in death.

Stag, exult on glen and mountain –
Salmon, leap from loch to fountain –
Heron, in the free air warm ye –
Uisneach's Sons no more will harm ye!

Erin's stay no more you are,
Rulers of the ridge of war;
Never more 'twill be your fate

Ulster

To keep the beam of battle straight.

Woe is me! by fraud and wrong –
Traitors false and tyrants strong –
Fell Clan Uisneach, bought and sold,
For Barach's feast and Conor's gold!

Woe to Eman, roof and wall! –
Woe to Red Branch, hearth and hall! –
Tenfold woe and black dishonour
To the false and foul Clan Conor!

Dig the grave both wide and deep,
Sick I am, and fain would sleep!
Dig the grave and make it ready,
Lay me on my true Love's body!

[*from the Irish*]

Sometime in the late 1960s I sat in an orange-grove in Pomona, California, listening humbly to a dissertation on Stephens and Ferguson and those Deirdre poems by another great poet, W.R. Rodgers. And what, you may ask, were two sons of Ulster doing under the oranges in sunny Pomona? D'Arcy O'Brien, novelist and professor, had organized a week of Irish literary studies with guests including Rodgers, Conor Cruise O'Brien and his wife Máire, the American academic Herbert Howarth, a sound authority on Irish literary matters, and, well down the ranks, myself.

W.R. (Bertie) went on to speak his own poem about another notable tragic lady:

LENT

Mary Magdalene, that easy woman,
Saw, from the shore, the seas
Beat against the hard stone of Lent,
Crying, 'Weep, seas, weep
For yourselves that cannot dent me more.

And as I Rode by Granard Moat

O more than all these, more crabbed than all stones,
And cold, make me, who once
Could leap like water, Lord. Take me
As one who owes
Nothing to what she was. Ah, naked.

My waves of scent, my petticoats of foam
Put from me and rebut;
Disown. And that salt lust stave off
That slavered me – O
Let it whiten in grief against the stones

And outer reefs of me. Utterly doff,
Nor leave the slightest veil
Of feeling to heave or soften.
Nothing cares this heart
What hardness crates it now or coffins.

Over the balconies of these curved breasts
I'll no more peep to see
The light procession of my loves
Surf-riding in to me
Who now have eyes and alcove, Lord, for Thee.'

'Room, Mary,' said He, 'ah make room for me
Who am come so cold now
To my tomb.' So, on Good Friday,
Under a frosty moon
They carried Him and laid Him in her womb.

A grave and icy mask her heart wore twice,
But on the third day it thawed,
And only a stone's-throw away
Mary saw her God.
Did you hear me? Mary saw her God!

Dance, Mary Magdalene, dance, dance and sing,
For unto you is born
This day a King. 'Lady,' said He,
'To you who relent
I bring back the petticoat and the bottle of scent.'

But I am still happy with Bertie in that orange-grove in Pomona.

I managed to quote to one Ulster poet a personal statement from another, Joseph Campbell.

I AM THE MOUNTAINY SINGER

I am the mountainy singer –
The voice of the peasant's dream,
The cry of the wind on the wooded hill,
The leap of the fish in the stream.

Quiet and love I sing –
The carn on the mountain crest,
The cailín in her lover's arms,
The child at its mother's breast.

Beauty and peace I sing –
The fire on the open hearth,
The cailleach spinning at her wheel,
The plough in the broken earth.

Travail and pain I sing –
The bride on the childing bed,
The dark man labouring at his rhymes,
The ewe in the lambing shed.

Sorrow and death I sing –
The canker come on the corn,
The fisher lost on the mountain loch,
The cry at the mouth of morn.

No other life I sing,
For I am sprung of the stock
That broke the hilly land for bread,
And built the nest in the rock!

Bertie responded with that most moving tribute to Belfast from the scholar Maurice Craig:

And as I Rode by Granard Moat

Red brick in the suburbs, white horse on the wall,
Eyetalian marbles in the City Hall:
O stranger from England, why stand so aghast?
May the Lord in His mercy be kind to Belfast.

This jewel that houses our hopes and our fears
Was knocked up from the swamp in the last hundred years;
But the last shall be first and the first shall be last:
May the Lord in His mercy be kind to Belfast.

We swore by King William there'd never be seen
An All-Irish Parliament at College Green,
So at Stormont we're nailing the flag to the mast:
May the Lord in His mercy be kind to Belfast.

O the bricks they will bleed and the rain it will weep,
And the damp Lagan fog lull the city to sleep;
It's to hell with the future and live on the past:
May the Lord in His mercy be kind to Belfast.

Then back we went, in our faraway talk, to Marshall, the Reverend, of Sixmilecross, recalling his epic in two poems about a tough old farmer by the name of Wee Robert:

SARAH ANN

I'll change me way of goin', for me head is gettin' grey,
I'm tormented washin' dishes, an' makin' dhraps o' tay;
The kitchen's like a midden, an' the parlour like a sty,
There's half a fut o' clabber on the street outby:
I'll go down agane the morra on me kailey to the Cross
For I'll hif to get a wumman, or the place'll go to loss.

I've fothered all the kettle, an' there's nothin' afther that
But clockin' roun' the ashes wi' an oul' Tom cat;
Me very ears is bizzin' from the time I light the lamp,
An' the place is like a graveyard, bar the mare wud give a stamp,
So often I be thinkin' an' conthrivin' for a plan
Of how to make the match agane with Robert's Sarah Ann.

Ulster

I used to make wee Robert's of a Sunday afther prayers,
– Sarah Ann wud fetch the taypot to the parlour up the stairs;
An' wance a week for sartin I'd be chappin' at the dure,
There wosn't wan wud open it but her, ye may be sure;
An' then – for all wos goin' well – I got a neighbour man
An' tuk him down to spake for me, an' ax for Sarah Ann.

Did ye iver know wee Robert? Well, he's nothin' but a wart,
A nearbegone oul' divil with a wee black heart,
A crooked, crabbit crathur that bees nether well nor sick,
Girnin' in the chimley corner, or goan happin' on a stick;
Sure ye min' the girl for hirin' that went shoutin' thro' the fair,
'I wunthered in wee Robert's, I can summer anywhere.'

But all the same wee Robert has a shap an' farm o' lan',
Ye'd think he'd do it dacent when it came to Sarah Ann,
She bid me axe a hundther'd, an' we worked him up and down,
The deil a hate he'd give her but a cow an' twenty poun';
I pushed for twenty more forbye to help to build a byre,
But ye might as well be talkin' to the stone behind the fire.

So says I till John, me neighbour, 'Sure we're only lossin' time,
Jist let him keep his mollye, I can do without her prime,
Jist let him keep his daughter, the hungry-lukin' nur,
There's jist as chancy weemin, in the countryside as her.'
Man, he let a big thravalley, an' sent us both – ye know,
But Sarah busted cryin', for she seen we maned till go.

Ay she fell till the cryin', for ye know she isn't young,
She's nearly past her market, but she's civil with her tongue.
That's half a year or thereaways, an' here I'm sittin' yit,
I'll change me way of goin', ay I'll do it while I'm fit,
She's a snug welldoin' wumman, no better in Tyrone,
An' down I'll go the morra, for I'm far too long me lone.

The night the win' is risin' an' it's comin' on to sleet,
It's spittin' down the chimley on the greeshig at me feet,
It's whistlin' at the windy, an' it's roarin' roun' the barn,
There'll be piles of snow the morra on more than Mullagharn;
But I'm for tacklin' Sarah Ann; no matter if the snow
Is iverywhere shebowin; when the morra comes I'll go.

And as I Rode by Granard Moat

THE RUNAWAY
[*A Sequel to 'Sarah Ann'*]

I towl yez afore about marryin'
How the notion come intil me head;
I wos livin' in dhurt an' amdasbut
I wos pushioned with tay an' white bread.
I wos puddlin' at shirts in a bucket,
I wos baffled with sarvints an' fowl,
An' wan night with me feet in the ashes
I rusted – I did, be my sowl.

Sarah Ann, sure yez heerd about her too,
But yez didn't hear more nor the half;
She's a fessend oul' thing, but her father
Wee Robert he's tarble well-aff.
But, boys, when I mentioned the fortune,
Ye'd a thought when the argymint riz
That he hadn't the nails for to scratch with,
He's as mane as get-out, so he is.

Well, he cooled in the skin he got hot in,
He got lave, the crookedoul' cowlt,
No fault till his daughter, I left her
But I foun' meself still in a howlt.
Sure the bread that I baked wos like concrete,
An' the butther – now I wud consate,
The man that can ate his own butther
There's nawthin' that man cudn't ate.

I'd a litther of pigs to sit up wi',
An' pigs is like Christians – man, dear,
Ye'd a thought they wor sthrivin' to tell me
'We're lost for a wumman up here.'
Calves died on me, too, in the spring-time,
The kettle got foundered in rain,
Hens clocked, or they took the disordher,
An' me heart warmed till Sarah agane.

So I went, an' if Robert wos hasky,
Sarah Ann wos as nice as cud be,
She done well, for who wud she get now?

Deil a wan if she didn't get me.
But her father had still lik a coolness,
Not wan word of welkim he dhrapt
Nor he nivir sayed what he wud give her,
He wos dotin', she sayed – he wos apt!

I got full in the June fair of Carmin,
I rid home, an' I met Sarah Ann,
– The thurf wos near ridy for clampin'
An' a wumman can give a good han' –
Sez I, 'Wull ye come for a half-wan?
Ye'll not. Well, listen to this.
Yon hirplin gazaybo, yir father,
He'll say nether ay, naw nor yis.'

So sez I, 'I'll not stan' it no longer,
Ye can take me or lave me, an' min'
Here's the cowlt can take me in the seddle,
With you an' yir bardhix behin'.
So come on now, or stan' there for iver,
Come on now, quet scratchin' your chin,
It's a runaway, that's what we'll make it,
Till Tamson's up there in Cloghfin.'

Sure I knowed she wud come, sure I knowed it.
Is it hir? Boys, she just made a bowlt,
Got a shawl an' whusked it about her,
Got stredlegs behin' on the cowlt.
Ay, stredlegs, for that's the way weemin
Bees ridin' the horses all now;
But heth, 'Twos an odd-lukin' runaway,
For the cowlt had to walk like a cow.

Oul' Tamson wos gled for to see us,
A' dacent, he done what wos right,
He sent for the dhrink an' the neighbours,
We had dancin' an' tay the whole night.
We got dhrunk, an' we fell till the fightin',
Be me sang oul' John's purty tyugh,
It wos prime how he leathered all roun' him
An' him jist as full as a shugh.

And as I Rode by Granard Moat

Big Jim ketched a howlt o' me whuskers,
Sez I, 'Ye can thry yirself, Jim,'
But me bowl Sarah Ann with a potstick
She soon lif her thrademark on him.
'Ye unsignified ghost!' sez his mother,
An' with that jist before he cud wink
She ketched Sarah Ann be the thrapple
An' whammeld her right in the sink.

When weemin gets wicked they're tarra,
Ye'll not intherfair if yir wise,
For ten townlans wudn't settle
The birl that two weemin can rise.
It wos nearly been that up in Tamson's,
We fought from the fire till the dure,
We fought – if ye'sdsay it wos fightin',
We fought in a heap on the flure.

That an' all we got grate afore mornin',
We wor frens throughother ye see;
John yocked just afther wir brekwis,
An' we stharted for Robert's, iz three.
But we nivir thought what we wor in for,
Heth naw, we dhrive up at a throt,
But the welkim wos sharp, 'twos a pitchfork,
An' that's all the welkim we got.

Boys, ye nivir seen sichin a han'lin,
I wos thunnersthruck wathchin' the birl,
The oul' da limpin' out wi' the pitchfork,
An' the frens makin' glam for the girl,
They dhregged her out over the tailboord,
She screamed, but I darn't intherfair,
An' they sliped her – aw lominty father,
They sliped her right in to the stair.

The gowls of wee Robert wos tarra,
The veins riz like coards on his skull,
'How dar ye? How dar ye? How dar ye?
I'll take ye to coort, so I wull.'
He miscalled me for all the oul' thurfmen,
All iver ye heerd he went through,

70

Ulster

Sez I, 'Ye may go till the bad place,
I'm as good jist as she is, or you.'

An' sez I, 'Me oul' boy, yir as ignornt,
As a pig let loose in a fair,'
Oul' Tamson broke in an' he toul' him
He cudn't fetch guts till a bear.
Well, boys, he wos frothin' with anger,
The spittles flew from him a parch,
But what good wos that? We wor done for,
We just had to lave him an' march.

I come home. I sot down in the kitchen,
Thinks I, 'I'll go through with it now,'
So I riz an' went back till oul' Tamson's
(He wos puttin' a ring in the sow),
An' sez I, 'I've a five naggin bottle,
Put a coat on ye, John, it's like rain,
Iz two'll go up to Long Francey's
An' tell him I'll take Liza Jane.'

Sez he, 'Ye've no call to be hasty,'
Sez I, 'Aw yis I hev call,
When the biz gets out through the country,
I'll not get a wumman at all.'
Sez he, 'Liza Jane – who wud she be?'
'The fat wan,' sez I, 'she can plow,'
'Be me sowl,' sez oul' John, 'it's a tarra,
But no matther, I'll go with ye now.'

So that's how I got me big wumman,
We settled it quick, so we did,
I'm content, she's a brave civil crathur,
An' quate, an' diz what she's bid.
Not hard to keep up, that's a good thing
When times isn't good on the lan',
She's young, but she's settled, an' more too,
She can work in the bog like a man.

She has no backspangs in her ether,
No harm in her more nor a hen,
If I take maybe wan or two half-wans

She nivir gets up on her en'.
Sarah Ann can now hannel a potstick,
If that's any affset – a mane
Takin' wan thing jist with the other
I'm thankful I picked Sarah Jane.

We talked then of our friend Michael J. Murphy, folklorist and storyteller, whose wonderful book *At Slieve Gullion's Foot* (1941) told of old ways and happier days. And we sang an old ballad we had first heard from Michael, its words as rough and unhewn as the rocks of that mythological mountain:

THE BOYS OF MULLAGHBAWN

On a Monday morning early my wandering steps did lead me
Down by a farmer's station, through meadows and green lawn,
Where I heard great lamentations the small birds they were making
Saying: 'We'll have no more engagements on the hills of Mullaghbawn.'

I beg your pardon ladies, and ask you as a favour,
I hope it is no treason now what I'm going to say.
I'm condoling late and early, my very heart is breaking
All for a noble lady that lives near Mullaghbawn.

Squire Jackson he is ranging for honour and for treasure,
He never did turn traitor nor betray the Rights of Man.
But now we are in danger by a wicked, deceiving stranger
Who has ordered transportation for the Boys of Mullaghbawn.

Far and near the seas were roaring, the billows they were flowing,
As those heroes crossed over I thought the sea would yawn.
The trout and salmon gaping, the cuckoo left her station,
Fare you well old Erin, and the Boys of Mullaghbawn.

These days, alas, there can be funny things going on around Mullaghbawn. But, far away in California, Bertie the Poet and myself had nothing but happy thoughts and we talked of that notable Ulsterman of music and balladry,

David Hammond, who had once written out for me two special verses about Old Ardboe on the Loughshore:

> You Gods assist my poor weary notion,
> You Inspired Muses lend me your hand,
> Till I exhort my quill without blot or blemish,
> Till I set forth the praises of this lovely strand
> That's well situated in the North of Ireland,
> Being all in the County of sweet Tyrone,
> Joining the banks of Lough Neagh's bright waters,
> Is that ancient fabric they call Old Ardboe.
>
> Now I stood in amazement to view the harbour
> Where the purling streams they do gently flow,
> Where the trout and salmon were nimbly sporting,
> Which brings more order to you, Old Ardboe.
> Now I've travelled Roosia and a part of Proosia,
> I have travelled Spain and all along the Rhine,
> But in all my rakings and undertakings
> Ardboe your equal I never could find.

And to bring us close to the last Irish refuge of the Great Hugh O'Neill, in Glanconkyne, on the border of Derry and Tyrone, Davy Hammond had also written out for me the praises of Wild Slieve Gallen Brae:

> Once I loved a damsel but, alas, she proved untrue,
> I thought to climb those mountains her cottage to view
> And whether it was magic or enchantment led the way
> Till at length I reached the summit of wild Slieve Gallen Brae.
>
> I thought to view her cottage, as Cupid led my heart,
> Or whether 'twould be better to rise up and to part
> Or to walk around with pleasure and let fancy guide the way,
> To view the works of Nature, on wild Slieve Gallen Brae.
>
> I viewed the groves and valleys along its rugged side,
> Likewise the stoney battery where timid rabbits hide,
> And the moorcock he kept crowing, the pleasures of that day
> All among the moss and heather on wild Slieve Gallen Brae.

And as I Rode by Granard Moat

As I sat down my limbs to rest, beyond yon pathless scar,
In view of many an object anear and afar,
The hills of County Antrim and the waters of Lough Neagh,
To me they shone like diamonds bright, from wild Slieve Gallen Brae.

Just over in the heather not very far away
I spied a lovely damsel fair a-stepping on her way,
Said I, 'My comely damsel what brought you here this day
Among this lonely wilderness of wild Slieve Gallen Brae?'

With slow hesitation her tale she thus began
Saying, 'Once I was deluded by a very false young man,
He promised he would marry me but he sailed across the say
And left me here to mourn and weep on wild Slieve Gallen Brae.'

II

From Ulster to Leinster

So you might say I had to go all the way to Pomona to begin to make my way out of Ulster, and then only to bring Ulster with me to an Ulster poet. So let us go south for a bit, and to go south we must cross the Boyne.

Sixty-six years ago, in the company of my father, I first made that crossing. As the train went over the great viaduct two decent men in our coach stood solemnly to attention. Afterwards my father explained to me that they did so in pious commemoration of another crossing upstream at Oldbridge. So in memory of those two men here are the words of the song as Halliday Sparling gave it in his *Irish Minstrelsy*, where he explains:

This version of the 'Boyne Water' is in universal use among the Orangemen of Ireland, and is the only one ever sung by them. But that it is not the original song, written nigh two centuries ago, is perfectly certain. Fragments of the old 'Boyne Water', as still remembered in the North, are next given.

> July the first in Oldbridge town,
> There was a grievous battle,
> Where many a man lay on the ground,
> By the cannons that did rattle.
> King James he pitched his tents between
> The lines for to retire;
> But King William threw his bomb-balls in,
> And set them all on fire.
>
> Thereat engaged they vowed revenge
> Upon King William's forces,

And as I Rode by Granard Moat

And often vehemently cried
That they would stop their courses;
A bullet from the Irish came,
Which grazed King William's arm,
They thought His Majesty was slain,
Yet it did him little harm.

Then Duke Schomberg he in friendly care,
His King would often caution
To shun the spot where bullets hot
Retained their rapid motion;
But William said, 'He don't deserve
The name of Faith's Defender,
Who would not venture life and limb
To make a foe surrender.'

When we the Boyne began to cross,
The enemy they descended;
But few of our brave men were lost,
So stoutly we defended;
The horse were the first that marched o'er,
The foot soon followed after;
But brave Duke Schomberg was no more,
By venturing over the water.

When valiant Schomberg he was slain,
King William then accosted
His warlike men for to march on
And he would be the foremost:
'Brave boys,' he said, 'be not dismayed,
For the losing of one Commander,
For God will be our King this day,
And I'll be the general under.'

Then stoutly we the Boyne did cross,
To give our enemies battle:
Our cannon, to our foe's great cost,
Like thundering claps did rattle;
In majestic mien our Prince rode o'er,
His men soon followed after,
With blow and shout put foes to the rout
The day we crossed the Water.

From Ulster to Leinster

The Protestants of Drogheda
Have reason to be thankful,
That they were not to bondage brought,
They being but a handful,
First to the Tholsel they were brought,
And tied at the Millmount after;
But brave King William set them free,
By venturing over the Water.

The cunning French near to Duleek
Had taken up their quarters,
And fenced themselves on every side,
Awaiting for new orders;
But in the dead time of the night
They set the fields on fire,
And long before the morning light
To Dublin they did retire.

Then said King William to his men,
After the French departed,
'I'm glad indeed that none of ye
Seemed to be faint-hearted;
So sheathe your swords and rest awhile
In time we'll follow after.'
Those words he uttered with a smile
The day he crossed the Water.

Come let us all with heart and voice
Applaud our lives' defender,
Who at the Boyne his valour showed
And made his foe surrender.
To God above the praise we'll give
Both now and ever after;
And bless the glorious Memory
Of William that crossed the Water.

But perhaps a better way to go to Dublin would be to travel on the train with Louis MacNeice, and afterwards to walk the city with him while he meditates on the delicate relationship between this strange city and a man from Ulster.

And as I Rode by Granard Moat

TRAIN TO DUBLIN

Our half-thought thoughts divide in sifted wisps
Against the basic facts repatterned without pause,
I can no more gather my mind up in my fist
Than the shadow of the smoke of this train upon the grass –
This is the way that animals' lives pass.

The train's rhythms never relent, the telephone posts
Go striding backwards like the legs of time to where
In a Georgian house you turn at the carpet's edge
Turning a sentence while, outside my window here,
The smoke makes broken queries in the air.

The train keeps moving and the rain holds off,
I count the buttons on the seat, I hear a shell
Held hollow to the ear, the mere
Reiteration of integers, the bell
That tolls and tolls, the monotony of fear.

At times we are doctrinaire, at times we are frivolous,
Plastering over the cracks, a gesture making good,
But the strength of us does not come out of us.
It is we, I think, are the idols and it is God
Has set us up as men who are painted wood,

And the trains carry us about. But not consistently so,
For during a tiny portion of our lives we are not in trains,
The idol living for a moment, not muscle-bound
But walking freely through the slanting rain,
Its ankles wet, its grimace relaxed again.

All over the world people are toasting the King,
Red lozenges of light as each one lifts his glass,
But I will not give you any idol or idea, creed or king,
I give you the incidental things which pass
Outward through space exactly as each was.

I give you the disproportion between labour spent
And joy at random; the laughter of the Galway sea
Juggling with spars and bones irresponsibly,
I give you the toy Liffey and the vast gulls,
I give you fuchsia hedges and whitewashed walls.

From Ulster to Leinster

I give you the smell of Norman stone, the squelch
Of bog beneath your boots, the red bog-grass,
The vivid chequer of the Antrim hills, the trough of dark
Golden water for the cart-horses, the brass
Belt of serene sun upon the lough.

And I give you the faces, not the permanent masks,
But the faces balanced in the toppling wave –
His glint of joy in cunning as the farmer asks
Twenty per cent too much, or a girl's, forgetting to be suave,
A tiro choosing stuffs, preferring mauve.

And I give you the sea and yet again the sea's
Tumultuous marble,
With Thor's thunder or taking his ease akimbo,
Lumbering torso, but finger-tips a marvel
Of surgeon's accuracy.

I would like to give you more but I cannot hold
This stuff within my hands and the train goes on;
I know that there are further syntheses to which,
As you have perhaps, people at last attain
And find that they are rich and breathing gold.

DUBLIN

Grey brick upon brick,
Declamatory bronze
On sombre pedestals –
O'Connell, Grattan, Moore –
And the brewery tugs and the swans
On the balustraded stream
And the bare bones of a fanlight
Over a hungry door
And the air soft on the cheek
And porter running from the taps
With a head of yellow cream
And Nelson on his pillar
Watching his world collapse.

This was never my town,
I was not born nor bred
Nor schooled here and she will not

79

And as I Rode by Granard Moat

Have me alive or dead
But yet she holds my mind
With her seedy elegance,
With her gentle veils of rain
And all her ghosts that walk
And all that hide behind
Her Georgian façades –
The catcalls and the pain,
The glamour of her squalor,
The bravado of her talk.

The lights jig in the river
With a concertina movement
And the sun comes up in the morning
Like barley-sugar on the water
And the mist on the Wicklow hills
Is close, as close
As the peasantry were to the landlord,
As the Irish to the Anglo-Irish,
As the killer is close one moment
To the man he kills,
Or as the moment itself
Is close to the next moment.

She is not an Irish town
And she is not English,
Historic with guns and vermin
And the cold renown
Of a fragment of Church latin
Of an oratorical phrase.
But O the days are soft,
Soft enough to forget
The lesson better learnt,
The bullet on the wet
Streets, the crooked deal,
The steel behind the laugh,
The Four Courts burnt.

Fort of the Dane,
Garrison of the Saxon,
Augustan capital
Of a Gaelic nation,

From Ulster to Leinster

Appropriating all
The alien brought,
You give me time for thought
And by a juggler's trick
You poise the toppling hour –
O greyness run to flower,
Grey stone, grey water
And brick upon grey brick.

On another and an older bagpipe, this is Dublin.

Oh, Dublin City, there is no doubting,
Bates every city upon the say.
'Tis there you'll hear O'Connell spouting
And see Lady Morgan makin' tay ...

For it is the capital of the finest nation
That ever grew on a fruitful sod,
Fightin' like divils for Conciliation
And hatin' each other for the love of God.

But perish that ancient and sardonic thought and let us
begin our tribute to Dublin right here where I stand, and sit,
and occasionally lie prostrate: in Donnybrook, where the
famous fair was established by King John of England. A long
time after that, while the fair was still functioning, its
Humours were celebrated by an anonymous balladeer:

To Donnybrook steer, all you sons of Parnassus,
Poor painters, poor poets, poor newsmen and knaves,
To see what the fun is, that all fun surpasses,
The sorrow and sadness of green Erin's slaves ...
O you lads that are witty, from famed Dublin city,
And you that in pastime take any delight,
To Donnybrook fly, for the time's drawing nigh
When fat pigs are hunted and lean cobblers fight,
When maidens, so swift, run for a new shift,
Men, muffled in sacks, for a shirt they race there,
There jockeys well-booted and horses sure-footed,
All keep up the Humours of Donnybrook Fair.

The mason does come with his line and his plumb,
The sawyer and carpenter, brothers in chips.
There are carvers and gilders and all sorts of builders,
With soldiers from barracks and sailors from ships.
There confectioners, cooks and printers of books,
There stampers of linen and weavers repair,
There widows and maids, and all sorts of trades
Go join in the Humours of Donnybrook Fair.

'Tis there are dogs dancing and wild beasts a-prancing,
With neat bits of painting in red, yellow and gold,
Toss-players and scramblers, and showmen and gamblers,
Pickpockets in plenty, both of young and of old.
There are brewers and bakers and jolly shoe-makers,
With butchers and porters and men that cut hair.
There are mountebanks grinning, while others are sinning
To keep up the Humours of Donnybrook Fair ...

John Keegan, the Laois poet (not to be confused with John Keegan Casey, who wrote 'The Rising of the Moon'), saw Donnybrook Fair somewhat differently. Keegan, a hedge-schoolmaster and of a family of much-devoted and ill-rewarded pedants, wrote verse and lamented for poor Pinch and Caoch O'Leary. He also wrote interesting prose fragments on folk-beliefs around Grantstown Lough in his part of the Midlands and elsewhere, collected into one volume by the notable Canon O'Hanlon, who wrote forever about the lives and doings of the saints of Ireland.

Keegan was morose and a misogynist and may have had good reason for his misery. Sometime before 1847 he saw Donnybrook Fair and this is what he thought:

I was two days and a piece of one night at Donnybrook Fair. I was told (and from previous description I believe it) that the fair this year was no more to the carnivals of other days than the puppet Punch is to the Colossus of Rhodes. Heaven knows, it would be a blessing if Donnybrook was sunk in hell and expunged forever from the map of our unfortunate country. I had conceptions of vice, of profligacy and debauchery, I had read Eugene Sue and Lytton Bulwer and George

Sand, but never did I dream of human debasement until I went to Donnybrook. In my opinion (and I try to be moderate), on last Thursday there were at least 40,000 females in Donnybrook: of these, I would be on my oath, there were at five o'clock in the evening, 30,000 more or less intoxicated ...

And on goes John, my dear ghost:

You tell me of Irish virtue. I once gloried in the dreams of Irish modesty, but, alas, in Donnybrook my eyes were opened. I was grieved, I was humbled, I was mortified. Indeed, I will never again go to Donnybrook or, if I do, I never again will mingle in the vortex of degraded human beings which unfortunately contribute the great mass of the meeting. I saw hundreds of ladies and gentlemen there, but unless the depraved portion of this class (and there are ladies enough depraved in Dublin), they remained in their carriages and cars, and did not mingle at all amongst the mob. But people of the highest rank go to see the fair.

Dear John, dear ghost, my suffering fellow Irishman, we know that you had your worries about women. They did not suit you, and I'm not blaming you for that. But thirty thousand drunken women between my garden gate and the bridge, three hundred yards away, over the River Dodder, dear John, I fear that you grossly exaggerate.

You were also, I grieve to note, a bit of a snob. All those ladies and gentlemen who came to study the drive-in movie from the safety of their horse-mobiles. May we hope that they enjoyed themselves and were proud of Donnybrook and the neighbouring town of Dublin: as was my dear friend Donagh MacDonagh, the son of Thomas MacDonagh:

> Dublin made me and no little town
> With the country closing in on its streets,
> The cattle walking proudly on its pavements,
> The jobbers, the gombeenmen and the cheats
>
> Devouring the fair day between them,
> A public-house to half a hundred men,
> And the teacher, the solicitor and the bank-clerk
> In the hotel bar, drinking for ten.

Dublin made me, not the secret poteen still,
The raw and hungry hills of the West,
The lean road flung over profitless bog
Where only a snipe could nest,

Where the sea takes its tithe of every boat.
Bawneen and curragh have no allegiance of mine,
Nor the cute, self-deceiving talkers of the South
Who look to the East for a sign.

The soft and dreary midlands with their tame canals
Wallow between sea and sea, remote from adventure,
And Northward a far and fortified province
Crouches under the lash of arid censure.

I disclaim all fertile meadows, all tilled land,
The evil that grows from it and the good,
But the Dublin of old statutes, this arrogant city,
Stirs proudly and secretly in my blood.

One of my most treasured possessions is a typescript copy of a comic verse-play, 'Down by the Liffey Side' by Donagh MacDonagh, presented to me by the author. Written as a send-up of Dion Boucicault and set in the Marshalsea prison for debtors, it has wonderful moments. Here you have, in the first verse, the high-class roisterer, the eternally hopeful gambler, the sad amorist, and then the Fourth Man: a hapless and ordinary citizen like yourself or myself; and all around them, the bustling life of the ancient prison. This scene closely resembles St Luke's Hospital as illustrated in Ackroyd's 'Microcosm of London'. William, without his wig, his lace soiled and torn, is sitting dejectedly on a bench while, around him, the other debtors drink, smoke and sing.

First Debtor
Behold the pauper's prison, the hell of bankrupt debtors,
Where sadly we're repenting for our spendthrift, happy days,
Remembering the bottles that emptied down our gullets,
The wigs, the lace, the satins and the ruinous displays.

From Ulster to Leinster

Oh, once I lived contentedly and friends I loved surrounded me;
Care nor grief ne'er troubled me nor made my heart feel sore,
But now those days are over and here I rot in misery,
Reflecting on the abstinence that fifty times I swore.

Debtors
Ochone, och ochone.

Second Debtor
'Twas dice that proved my downfall, the cards and little horses
Whose speed was far inferior to every other horse;
The fly I had my cash on alighted last invariably;
My raindrop on the window panes dried up, nor stayed the course;
But were I rich and young again and could I all I'd lost regain,
I'd live the same life out again, and luck would turn my way;
With dice and cards and claret the night would vanish rapidly
And I would rise triumphant at the closing of the play.

Debtors
Ochone, och ochone.

Third Debtor
A dark eye or a grey eye, an eye that's soft and tender,
A form that's tall and slender, a breast that stands at bay,
An ankle trim and shapely, a hand that's slim and playful,
A mouth that's shaped for kissing and breath that's a bouquet,
These are the charms that ruined me, yet I pursued them foolishly,
Certain that each new schooling would give me my degree;
But all a lifetime brought me the first girl could have taught me,
For all I ever learned of them was what they thought of me.

Debtors
Ochone, och ochone.

Fourth Debtor
I've never squandered money for I never had a penny,
I've never gambled madly, I was never drunk on wine,
The girls I had cost nothing except a bit of flattery,
Yet here I am in company that once was rich and fine.
I've hunted for prosperity, but still she has eluded me,
For bleak misfortune follows me no matter where I roam;
If I had had your fortunes I might be great and proud today,
Instead of sitting in the straw singing och, och ochone.

And as I Rode by Granard Moat

Debtors
Ochone, och ochone.

The TURNKEY enters and pushes the DEBTORS roughly out of his way.

Turnkey
Out of the way and be silent, you scum.
There are ladies approaching this villainous slum.
[to a DEBTOR] You owe me a crown for your bed and your board,
Bread and water, me boyo, is all you can afford.
[to the others] Jump to it and tidy this pigsty of yours,
And bow when you answer, you caricatures.
You bankrupt incompetents, I'll teach you to work ...
Ten strokes on the back for the first man to shirk.

But let us move on rapidly to a happier Dublin and one much closer to our own time. This would have been the Stillorgan Road, say, in the early 1940s, as the poet Roibeard Ó Faracháin saw it, before automobiles had completely taken over; anyway, the Second World War was on and petrol was not plentiful.

AUTUMN AFTERNOON

To think that a thing
as thoughtless as grass
could bring like a sting
the thought that there was

on ruggedy acorn,
horny nut,
on bead-bright berry,
fleshly fruit,
on pine-cone, gourd
– and grass of course –
a gloss!

On every other thing was there
a twinkle or a copper glare.
Trout would leap and crouch and linger.
O King Nuada's silver finger!
(Lost a hand. With the metal thing
ducked the law and stayed a king.)

From Ulster to Leinster

The weeshy Dodder-water's top
was satinwood, and the butcher's shop
a glimmering glass that shone and shone
and steel too hot to look upon:
you had to screw your eyes to look
where Something blazed upon a hook.

And on the smooth Stillorgan road,
where half the wheels in Ireland glowed,
the streamlined steel and vulcanite
were slithery with glinting light.

Riding their bicycles aflash
ladies were ladyly abashed
when frocks bob-bobbed
and, ducking the breeze,
went rippling back
from their glossy knees.
The polished legs of ladies glint
like guineas from an ancient mint
when knees arch up: they sleek like seals
when silk is straight from hams to heels:
ballet put on in crystal air
by switches of blackthorn sleekly bare.
Who would have thought a bike was bright
and sharp as a sculptured stalactite?
Or dreamed that the underwater green
of a beechleaf could turn tangerine?
Haws, coming crimson out, could flush
whitethorn into a burning bush?

Who was prepared for this (so soon)
enchanting Autumn afternoon?

Round about 1935 I was, very briefly, an actor. Hollywood
didn't hear about me so the matter never went further. But I
was in two stage plays in Omagh Town Hall, as a small part
of the Omagh Players. One of these was Padraic Gregory's
The Coming of the Magi, and I was one of the Magi, very
wise for my years. Padraic came to see us and advise us, and

even travelled with us when we went on tour all the thirty-four miles to Derry. He was a small man with delicate features and silver-white hair, and a dark coat with a Chestertonian cape. I find him here happy among the dancing children on the streets of Dublin:

DUBLIN'S CHILDREN

You've niver seen in all your lives the crowds o' little childher
Ye'll see the while ye bustle thro' the streets o' Dublin Town;
To count them all, 'tis my belief, it sorely would bewilder
The grandest scholar ye cud find in Ireland, up or down.

On Days o' Obligation or on Sundays from the Masses
Ye'll see them rompin' out in hundreds, chatterin' gay an' free,
On week-days, see the bigger ones go trudgin' to their classes,
Wi' fresh-washed faces, boots well-polished, staid as staid can be.

You'll see some wealthy childher (wi' their Da an' Ma go'n shoppin')
A-drivin' in to Dame Street from self-satisfied Rathgar,
An' chubby back-street urchins o'er the pavements come a-hoppin'
To gaze at them that loll like lords inside a glistenin' car.

You'll see some ragged youngster – hardly more than fit to toddle –
A-carryin' the baby o' the family in a shawl
(Her mother's out at work so she's to larn to nurse an' coddle)
Before she knows jist what it's like to be a child at all.

There's nurse-attended babies that are wheeled in spotless pramcars,
There's sturdy-legged two-year-olds that use their own wee feet,
An' laughin' crowin' infants in their mothers' arms in tramcars,
An' whiles, odd whiles, ye'll see a lost child cryin' in the street.

There's rosy-cheeked, an' pallid cheeked, an' bunty, fat an' slim ones,
Some that's grimy, some half-clean, an' some as white as snow,
There's healthy, weakly, surly, happy, sober-faced an' prim ones;
All sorts an' shapes o' boys and girls, no matter where ye go.

There's handsome, ugly, roguish ones, an' dark-haired, red an' fair ones,
Deep-blue-eyed lasses, impish lads wi' eyes as black as sloes,
There's fly, an' sly, an' rough an' tough, an' 'divil-a-hair-I-care' ones,
Where all those different childher come from – Heaven only knows.

There's quiet ones, an' boisterous ones wi' joy o' life jist bubblin',
Sedate, well-bred, or cheeky ones that pull each other's hair,
Throughout the whole o' Dublin, the pulsin' heart o' Dublin,
The great glad heart o' Dublin, shure there's childher everywhere.

Dublin, like many another city and town, has grown, for good or ill, over the years. Twenty years ago a friend of mine, an historical man and an authority on Old Dublin, came walking with me on the Hill of Killenarden. We walked up and up from Jobstown and over the Hill of Killenarden, looking from there on into Glenasmole, the Glen of the Thrushes, well praised by Patrick Pearse. And we recalled the verses written faraway beyond the ocean by Charles G. Halpine, a Kilkennyman, who got into some difficulties around about 1848. The hill Halpine wrote about, and the flat land all below it, is now part of the new suburbia. But Halpine, the Young Irelander, would be happy to see fine homes on good ground for the people of Ireland.

THE HILL OF KILLENARDEN

Though time effaces memory, and griefs the bosom harden,
I'll ne'er forget, where'er I be, that day at Killenarden;
For there, while fancy revelled wide, the summer's day flew o'er me;
The friends I loved were at my side, and Irish fields before me.

The road was steep; the pelting showers had cooled the sod beneath us;
And there were lots of mountain flowers, a garland to enwreath us.
Far, far below the landscape shone with wheat, and new-mown
   meadows,
And as o'erhead the clouds flew on, beneath swept on their shadows.

O friends, beyond the Atlantic's foam there may be noble mountains,
And in our new far western home green fields and brighter fountains;
But as for me, let time destroy all dreams, but this one pardon,
And barren memory long enjoy that day on Killenarden.

Round about fifty years ago I settled in Dublin city, and by virtue of being what used to be called a 'working journalist', had the right of entering the circle based in the Palace Bar, and later in the Pearl, around the renowned editor of *The Irish Times*, R.M. Smyllie. His weekly book-page, under the guidance of Bruce Williamson, carried every Saturday a new poem, and in 1944 Donagh MacDonagh made a selection of these under the simple title: *Poems from Ireland*.

It is a book I will always treasure. To me, no matter where or what those poems are about, the book smells and tastes and sings to me of my early and happy days as a Dubliner. But here, tucked inside the strong brown paper with which I have rebound the book, I find two yellowed newspaper clippings, both of book reviews. One, from 1958, has the poet Austin Clarke reviewing the poet Patrick MacDonogh; but let Patrick speak for himself out of the collection made by his fellow poet and namesake:

SHE WALKED UNAWARE

O, she walked unaware of her own increasing beauty
That was holding men's thoughts from market or plough,
As she passed by intent on her womanly duties
And she without leisure to be wayward or proud;
Or if she had pride then it was not in her thinking
But thoughtless in her body like a flower of good breeding.
The first time I saw her spreading coloured linen
Beyond the green willow she gave me gentle greeting
With no more intention than the leaning willow tree.

Though she smiled without intention yet from that day forward
Her beauty filled like water the four corners of my being,
And she rested in my heart like a hare in the form
That is shaped to herself. And I that would be singing
Or whistling at all times went silently then;
Till I drew her aside among straight stems of beeches
When the blackbird was sleeping and she promised that never
The fields would be ripe but I'd gather all sweetness,
A red moon of August would rise on our wedding.

October is spreading bright flame among stripped willows,
Low fires of the dogwood burn down to grey water, –

God pity me now and all desolate sinners
Demented with beauty! I have blackened my thought
In drouths of bad longing, and all brightness goes shrouded
Since he came with his rapture of wild words that mirrored
Her beauty and made her ungentle and proud.
To-night she will spread her brown hair on his pillow,
But I shall be hearing the harsh cries of wild fowl.

The second clipping dates from the August of 1974, and
has Seamus Heaney writing about the poems of Padraic
Fallon, the Dolmen Press volume of that year. One great, and
generous, poet writes about another, beginning his review:

Padraic Fallon has lived in important places where his mind kept
growing bold as light in Greece – and if I begin by crossing Kavanagh
on Clarke, it is not only to place Padraic Fallon within his poetic
generation, but also to suggest that his gifts combine certain kinds of
strength these two very different poets possessed separately, and that his
achievement in some way enhances theirs. I feel these poems, which
arrive like a windfall or a legacy, supply a missing link in the tradition of
Irish poetry since Yeats ...

We all know what Yeats had to say about the echoes and
the ghost of Blind Raftery, and the crossroads of Kiltartan,
and the bridge and the tower of Ballylee. Yet I feel that
Yeats would have accepted with a grave nod of the head
what Padraic Fallon had to say about all that and more.

MARY HYNES
(After the Irish of Raftery)

That Sunday, on my oath, the rain was a heavy overcoat
On a poor poet, and when the rain began
In fleeces of water to buckleap like a goat
I was only a walking penance reaching Kiltartan;
And there, so suddenly that my cold spine
Broke out on the arch of my back like a rainbow,
This woman surged out of the day with so much sunlight
I was nailed there like a scarecrow,

But I found my tongue and the breath to balance it
And I said: 'If I bow to you with this hump of rain
I'll fall on my collarbone, but look, I'll chance it,
And after falling, bow again.'
She laughed, ah, she was gracious, and softly she said to me,
'For all your lovely talking I go marketing with an ass,
I'm no hill-queen, alas, or Ireland, that grass widow,
So hurry on, sweet Raftery, or you'll keep me late for Mass!'

The parish priest has blamed me for missing second Mass
And the bell talking on the rope of the steeple,
But the tonsure of the poet is the bright crash
Of love that blinds the irons on his belfry,
Were I making an Aisling I'd tell the tale of her hair,
But now I've grown careful of my listeners
So I pass over one long day and the rainy air
Where we sheltered in whispers.

When we left the dark evening at last outside her door,
She lighted a lamp though a gaming company
Could have sighted each trump by the light of her unshawled poll,
And indeed she welcomed me
With a big quart bottle and I mooned there over glasses
Till she took that bird, the phœnix, from the spit;
And 'Raftery,' says she, 'a feast is no bad dowry,
Sit down now and taste it!'

If I praised Ballylee before it was only for the mountains
Where I broke horses and ran wild,
And not for its seven crooked smoky houses
Where seven crones are tied
All day to the listening top of a half door,
And nothing to be heard or seen
But the drowsy dropping of water
And a gander on the green.

But, Boys! I was blind as a kitten till last Sunday.
This town is Earth's very navel!
Seven palaces are thatched there of a Monday,
And O the seven queens whose pale
Proud faces with their seven glimmering sisters,
The Pleiads, light the evening where they stroll,

From Ulster to Leinster

And one can find the well by their wet footprints,
And make one's soul;

For Mary Hynes, rising, gathers up there
Her ripening body from all the love stories;
And, rinsing herself at morning, shakes her hair
And stirs the old gay books in libraries;
And what shall I do with sweet Boccaccio?
And shall I send Ovid back to school again
With a new headline for his copybook,
And a new pain?

Like a nun she will play you a sweet tune on a spinet,
And from such grasshopper music leap
Like Herod's hussy who fancied a saint's head
For grace after meat;
Yet she'll peg out a line of clothes on a windy morning
And by noonday put them ironed in the chest,
And you'll swear by her white fingers she does nothing
But take her fill of rest.

And I'll wager now that my song is ended,
Loughrea, that old dead city where the weavers
Have pined at the mouldering looms since Helen broke the thread,
Will be piled again with silver fleeces:
O the new coats and big horses! The raving and the ribbons!
And Ballylee in hubbub and uproar!
And may Raftery be dead if he's not there to ruffle it
On his own mare, Shank's mare, that never needs a spur!

But ah, Sweet Light, though your face coins
My heart's very metals, isn't it folly without pardon
For Raftery to sing so that men, east and west, come
Spying on your vegetable garden?
We could be so quiet in your chimney corner –
Yet how could a poet hold you anymore than the sun,
Burning in the big bright hazy heart of harvest,
Could be tied in a henrun?

Bless your poet then and let him go!
He'll never stack a haggard with his breath:
His thatch of words will not keep rain or snow

Out of the house, or keep back death.
But Raftery, rising, curses as he sees you
Stir the fire and wash delph,
That he was bred a poet whose selfish trade it is
To keep no beauty to himself.

In this same collection Robert Farren, who was always
much devoted to Dublin, casts his imagination as far away as
Dunquin in County Kerry:

THE WESTERN WORLD

Not a sinner in Dunquin
recollects John Synge –
'that meditative man, John Synge';
Cumeenole to Ballyferriter,
they've 'never heard of him.'

I wonder, if I went enquiring
through the stone-piled Aran Islands,
round Glenmalure or Glenmacnass,
Kippure or Lough Nahanagan,
would there any remember him,
any have heard of him?

That meditative man, John Synge,
like the catgut and silken string
he brought out of France or Spain
and fingered for Maurice Keane,
is snapt, scrapped and unstrung,
is cast down in the dung;
the fiddle come-over from France
makes none in Beg-Innish dance;
the birdcatcher left no mark
on the sod of his lark.

That violent man, James Lynchehaun,
left sagas in Achill;
that mite of a man, O Crihan,
yarns Ireland to the Blaskets;
but Synge's reverberant name –

like young men of Aran,
young girls of the Blaskets –
took ship from the Western World,
and has never returned.

Know you, child, that this great fool had laughter in his
heart and eyes: a million echoes, distant thence, since Dublin
taught him to be wise ...

That was Patrick Kavanagh, as I first knew him, back in
1941, when he was, like myself, walking the streets of
Dublin, doing a bit for the papers, being reasonably happy
and wondering what it was all about. But here is Patrick
looking back to his memory of the spraying of the potatoes
on the stony, grey soil of Monaghan; and then ascending in
one of the great devotional poems: devoted to all goodness
in humanity and to what, if anything, may live above:

SPRAYING THE POTATOES

The barrels of blue potato-spray
Stood on a headland of July
Beside an orchard wall where roses
Were young girls swinging from the sky.

The flocks of green potato-stalks
Were blossom-spread for sudden flight;
The Arran Banners wearing blue,
The Kerrs Pinks in a frivelled white.

And over that potato field
A lazy veil of woven sun;
Dandelions growing on headlands, showing
Their unpraised hearts to everyone.

And I was there with a knapsack sprayer
On the barrel's edge poised. A wasp was floating
Dead on a withered briar-leaf
Over a copper-poisoned ocean.

The axle-roll of a rut-locked cart
Broke the burnt stick of noon in two.

And as I Rode by Granard Moat

An old man came through a cornfield
Remembering his youth and the Ruth he knew.

He turned my way. 'God further the work.'
He echoed an ancient farming prayer.
I thanked him. He eyed the potato drills.
He said: 'You're bound to have good ones there.'

We talked, and our talk was a theme of kings,
A theme for strings. He hunkered down
In the shade of the orchard wall. O roses,
The old man dies in the young girl's frown.

And poet lost to potato fields,
Remembering the lime and copper smell
Of the spraying mixture, he is not lost,
Or till blossomed stalks cannot weave a spell.

RENEWAL

We have tested and tasted too much, lover –
Through a chink too wide there comes in no wonder.
But here in this Advent-darkened room
Where the dry black bread and the sugarless tea
Of penance will charm back the luxury
Of a child's soul we'll return to Doom
The knowledge we stole but could not use.

And the newness that was in every stale thing
When we looked at it as children: the spirit-shocking
Wonder in a black slanting Ulster hill
Or the prophetic astonishment in the tedious talking
Of an old fool will awake for us and bring
You and me to the yard-gate to watch the whins
And the bog-holes, cart-tracks, old stables where Time begins.

O after Christmas we'll have no need to go searching
For the difference that sets an old phrase burning –
We'll hear it in the whispered argument of a churning
Or in the streets where the village boys are lurching
And we'll hear it among simple decent men too
Who barrow dung in gardens under trees,
Wherever life pours ordinary plenty.

From Ulster to Leinster

Won't we be rich, my love and I, and please
God we shall not ask for Reason's payment,
The why of heart-breaking strangeness in dreeping hedges
Nor analyse God's breath in common statement.
We have thrown into the dust-bin the clay-minted wages
Of pleasure, knowledge and the conscious hour.
And Christ comes with a January flower.

But we are, at the moment, in Dublin city, and I hear
Valentin Iremonger celebrating an encounter with spring in
a Dublin suburb:

SPRING STOPS ME SUDDENLY

Spring stops me suddenly like ground
Glass under a door, squeaking and gibbering.
I put my hand to my cheek and the tips
Of my fingers feel blood pulsing and quivering.

A bud on a branch brushes the back
Of my hand and I look, without moving, down.
Summer is there, screwed and fused, compressed,
Neat as a bomb, its casing a dull brown.

From the window of a farther tree I hear
A chirp and a twitter; I blink.
A tow-headed vamp of a finch on a branch
Cocks a roving eye, tips me the wink.

And, instantly, the whole great hot-lipped ensemble
Of birds and birds, of clay and glass doors,
Reels in with its ragtime chorus, staggering
The theme of the time, a jam-session's rattle and roar

With drums of summer jittering in the background
Dully and, deeper down and more human, the sobbing
Oboes of autumn falling across the track of the tune,
Winter's furtive bassoon like a sea-lion snorting and bobbing.

There is something here I do not get,
Some menace that I do not comprehend,
Yet, so intoxicating is the song,
I cannot follow its thought right to the end.

So up the garden path I go with Spring
Promising sacks and robes to rig my years
And a young girl to gladden my heart in a tartan
Scarf and freedom from my facile fears.

That great novelist Francis Stuart has never made a secret of his passion for the spectacle and excitement of the running horses. Here he is recording his admiration for a racehorse carefully observed on the Curragh of Kildare:

A RACEHORSE AT THE CURRAGH

I see her poised upon the four smooth hooves;
The hind legs stretch a little from the body
In one taut line that, like the line of a bow,
Curves to the feathered dart. As on wet rooves
Glistens the sunlight, on the silken skin
It flickers, as if half-hidden sinews throw
The strain up to the raised, expectant head.

I see her walk upon the summer grass
And the faint move of muscles under a coat
That turns from violent copper almost to mauve;

Then suddenly the head's thrown up, the forelegs double
And the veiled speed is loosed
Into a bright shadow past our eyes,
Till, streaming neck outstretched, the hollow clap
Of flying hooves grows faint in the far distance.
And gazing after her I hear my heart
Beat as though stirred to quicker life again.

And now that we are into this romantic business of running horses and mares, let me give you a ballad to take with you to the Curragh, or Epsom or Longchamps or Newmarket or Kentucky.

(By the way, is there a ballad about the Curragh Races? There must be, but I never heard one. There is a sweet song about a fellow who, because of a broken heart, enlisted in

the British Army, but this makes only one brief reference to
the Curragh ...)

MY LOVE IS LIKE THE SUN

The winter is past,
And the summer's come at last
And the blackbirds sing on every tree;
The hearts of these are glad
But my poor heart is sad,
Since my true love is absent from me.

The rose upon the briar
By the water running clear
Gives joy to the linnet and the bee;
Their little hearts are blest
But mine is not at rest,
While my true love is absent from me.

A livery I'll wear
And I'll comb out my hair,
And in velvet so green I'll appear
And straight I will repair
To the Curragh of Kildare
For it's there I'll find tidings of my dear.

I'll wear a cap of black
With a frill around my neck,
Gold rings on my fingers I'll wear:
All this I'll undertake
For my true lover's sake,
He resides at the Curragh of Kildare.

I would not think it strange
Thus the world for to range
If I only get tidings of my dear;
But here in Cupid's chain
If I'm bound to remain,
I would spend my whole life in despair.

My love is like the sun
That in the firmament does run,

And always proves constant and true;
But he is like the moon
That wanders up and down,
And every month it is new.

All ye that are in love
And cannot it remove,
I pity the pains you endure;
For experience lets me know
That your hearts are full of woe,
And a woe that no mortal can cure.

No one knows who wrote that lovely song. Where are they now, the nameless authors of old sweet songs? Waiting for us in the shadows of eternity.

Nor, so far as I am aware, does anyone know who wrote the magnificent ballad about the Races of Bellewstown Hill, up above Laytown, where they horse-raced on the sands of the sea. It was written in 1860 by John Costello, editor of *The Drogheda Argus,* to celebrate the opening of 'the new Monolithic Stand', built by R.B. Daly of Drogheda to replace 'a wooden, rickety structure' which stood near the Duleek bend on the racecourse.

If respite you'd borrow from turmoil or sorrow,
I'll tell you the secret of how it is done.
'Tis found in this statement of all the excitement
That Bellewstown knows when the Races come on.
Make one of a party whose spirits are hearty,
Get a seat on a trap that is safe not to spill.
In its well pack a hamper, then off for a scamper,
And Huroo for the Glories of Bellewstown Hill.

On the road how they dash on, Rank, Beauty and Fashion,
It Banagher bangs, by the table of war,
From the coach of the Quality down to the Jollity
Joggin' along on an old low-backed car.
Though straw cushions are placed, two feet thick at the laste,
Its jigging and jogging to mollify, still

From Ulster to Leinster

The cheeks of my Nelly are shakin' like jelly
From the joltin' she gets as she jogs to the Hill.

In the tents play the pipers, the fiddlers and fifers,
Those rollicking lilts such as Ireland best knows.
While Paddy is prancing, his colleen is dancing
Demure, with her eyes quite intent on her toes.
More power to you Micky, faith your foot isn't sticky,
But bounds from the boards like a pen from the quill.
Oh, 'twould cure a rheumatic, he would jump up ecstatic
At Tatter Jack Walsh upon Bellewstown Hill.

Oh, 'tis there 'neath the haycocks all splendid like paycocks
In chattering groups that the Quality dine.
Sitting cross-legged like tailors the gentlemen dalers
In flattering spout and come out mighty fine.
And the gentry from Navan and Cavan are havin'
'Neath the shade of the trees an Arcadian quadrille.
All we read in the pages of pastoral ages
Tells of no scene like this upon Bellewstown Hill.

Arrived at the summit, the view that you come at
From etherealized Mourne to where Tara ascends,
There's no scene in our sireland, dear Ireland, old Ireland,
To which Nature more exquisite loveliness lends.
And the soil 'neath your feet has a memory sweet
The patriot's deeds they hallow it still
Eighty-two's Volunteers (would today see their peers?)
Marched past in review upon Bellewstown Hill.

But hark there's a shout, the horses are out
'Long the ropes on the strand what a hullabaloo.
To old Crockafotha the people that dot the
Broad plateau around are off for a view.
Come Ned, my tight fellow, I'll bet on the Yellow,
Success to the Green, we will stand by it still.
The uplands and hollows they're skimming like swallows
Till they flash by the post upon Bellewstown Hill.

A friend from Ardcath, County Meath, compiled a comprehensive account of old Bellewstown from many and varied sources. He had actual racecards from shortly after the

Battle of the Boyne, when the Cromwellian and Williamite planters revived the racing event, which had lapsed in the troubled centuries following the Anglo-Norman invasion. The Curragh had similarly gone into the darkness. There was evidence that Bellewstown was contemporary with, if not older than, the famous Kildare event and that racing and hunting went on there with Fionn and Na Fianna in the third century, when they also cavorted around the Curragh. As far back as the Bronze Age the Ard Rí came over from Tara to hunt and sport on Bellewstown Hill. The Bellews had not yet arrived.

But Bellewstown Hill was also, in more recent times, a Place of Assembly, as the ballad mentions in passing. Grattan's Volunteers marched there in July 1781, and Charlemont, accompanied by his aides, the Duke of Leinster and Henry Grattan MP, reviewed three thousand troops – horse, foot and artillery. And in 1843 Bellewstown had its Great Repeal Demonstration with twenty thousand people present.

On the way into Dublin we passed that way and saw never a ghost.

Since we are here in Dublin let us try for something of the ancient flavour of the place, and recall the good man by the name of Larry who went to meet his Maker in full view of the populace of the city:

THE NIGHT BEFORE LARRY WAS STRETCHED

The night before Larry was stretched,
The boys they all paid him a visit;
A bait in their sacks, too, they fetched;
They sweated their duds till they riz it:
For Larry was ever the lad,
When a boy was condemned to the squeezer,
Would fence all the duds that he had

From Ulster to Leinster

To help a poor friend to a sneezer,
And warm his gob 'fore he died.

The boys they came crowding in fast,
They drew all their stools round about him,
Six glims round his trap-case were placed,
He couldn't be well waked without 'em.
When one of us asked could he die
Without having duly repented?
Says Larry, 'That's all in my eye;
And first by the clergy invented,
To get a fat bit for themselves.'

'I'm sorry, dear Larry,' says I
'To see you in this situation;
And blister my limbs if I lie,
I'd as lieve it had been my own station.'
'Ochone! it's all over,' says he,
'For the neckcloth I'll be forced to put on,
And by this time to-morrow you'll see
Your poor Larry as dead as a mutton,
Because, why, his courage was good.

'And I'll be cut up like a pie,
And my nob from my body be parted.'
'You're in the wrong box, then,' says I,
'For blast me if they're so hard-hearted:
A chalk on the back of your neck
Is all that Jack Ketch dares to give you;
Then mind not such trifles a feck,
For why should the likes of them grieve you?
And now, boys, come tip us the deck.'

The cards being called for, they played,
Till Larry found one of them cheated;
A dart at his napper he made
(The boy being easily heated):
'O by the hokey, you thief,
I'll scuttle your nob with my daddle!
You cheat me because I'm in grief,
But soon I'll demolish your noddle,
And leave you your claret to drink.'

Then the clergy came in with his book,
He spoke him so smooth and so civil;
Larry tipped him a Kilmainham look,
And pitched his big wig to the devil;
Then sighing, he threw back his head
To get a sweet drop of the bottle,
And pitiful sighing, he said,
'O the hemp will be soon round my throttle,
And choke my poor windpipe to death.

'Though sure it's the best way to die,
O the devil a better a–livin'!
For when the gallows is high
Your journey is shorter to heaven:
But what harasses Larry the most,
And makes his poor soul melancholy,
Is that he thinks of the time when his ghost
Will come in a sheet to sweet Molly;
O sure it will kill her alive!'

So moving these last words he spoke,
We all vented our tears in a shower;
For my part, I thought my heart broke,
To see him cut down like a flower.
On his travels we watched him next day;
O the throttler, I thought I could kill him;
But Larry not one word did say,
Nor changed till he come to King William,
Then, musha, his colour grew white.

When he came to the nobbling chit,
He was tucked up so neat and so pretty,
The rumbler jogged off from his feet,
And he died with his face to the city;
He kicked, too – but that was all pride,
For soon you might see 'twas all over;
Soon after the noose was untied,
And at darkee we waked him in clover,
And sent him to take a ground sweat.

That extraordinary Corkman Francis Sylvester Mahony took
many liberties with people's names, beginning with that of
Father Prout, the quiet and inoffensive parish priest of

Watergrasshill on the road to Cork city. In one of his learned considerations in *Fraser's Magazine,* London, and under the title of 'The Songs of France', he attributed the above elegy, or threnody, to the Rev. Robt Burrowes, Dean of St Finbar's Cathedral, Cork. But Mahony, or Father Prout, claimed that the Rev. Burrowes had borrowed the masterpiece from a French original entitled 'La Mort de Socrate' by 'L'Abbé de Prout, Curé de Mont-aux-Cressons, près de Cork'. He went on to give the French version, the first verse of which reads:

> A la veille d'être perdu,
> Notre Laurent reçu dans son gîte,
> Honneur qui lui était bien dú,
> De nombreux amis la visite;
> Car chacun scavait que Laurent
> A son tour rendrait la pareille,
> Chapeau montre, et veste engageant,
> Pour que l'ami, put boire, bouteille
> Ni faire, à gosier sec, le saut.

Sing that, if you dare. And there are six more verses.

Brinsley MacNamara, novelist and playwright, took a devilish delight in these translations – or, as Mahony called them, 'Upsettings' – and I recall him dissertating on Mahony as the two of us walked the old Boyne Navigation towing-path from Navan to Slane. Brinsley was in the habit of doing that walk with his dear friend F.R. Higgins, who made the walk and the Meath man Brinsley matter for his poem 'The Boyne Walk'.

> 'What's all this rich land,' said I to the Meath man,
> 'Just mirrors bedazzled with blazing air!'
> And like flies on mirrors my parched thoughts ran
> As we walked, half-hidden, through where the reeds stand
> Between the Boyne and its green canal;
> And sweltering I kept to the pace he planned,

And as I Rode by Granard Moat

Yet he wouldn't even wait in the reeds
To watch a red perch, like a Japanese hand,
Grope in the sun-shot water and weeds –
He merely called back: 'O, go be damned!'

With break-neck looks at the withered end
Of a stupefied town, I paced his heel
By moat, dead wall and under an arch
That was all of a crouch with the weight of the years;
But where the road led I'd have seen – were I wise –
From one running look in the dark of his eyes:
For each seemed the bright astrological plan
Of a new Don Quixote and his man
Again on campaign; but lacking their steeds,
I'd sooner have seen a flick of grey ears
Or a blue lackadaisical eye in the reeds
To lead to a smoky bare back; then cheers!
We'd have ridden our road as the Kings of Meath.

We walked, as became two kings outcast
From plains walled in by a grass-raising lord,
Whose saint is the Joker, whose hope is the Past –
What victuals for bards could that lad afford?
O, none! So off went his dust from our boots,
But his dust that day was of buttercup gold
From a slope, with a sight that was, man alive, grand:
Just two servant girls spreading blue clothes
On grass too deep for a crow to land;
And though they waved to us we kept on our track,
And though to the bank their own clothes soon toppled
We sweltered along – while my thoughts floated back
Through shy beauty's bathing-pool, like an old bottle!

Heat trembled in halos on grass and on cattle
And each rock blazed like a drunken face;
So I cried to the man of the speedy wattle
'In the name of Lot's wife will you wait a space?
For Adam's red apple hops dry in my throttle,'
And yet instead of easing the pace,
I saw on the broad blackboard of his back
His muscles made signs of a far greater chase,

Until as I tried to keep up on his track
Each pore of my skin became a hot spring
And every bone swam in a blister of pains
While all my bent body seemed as an old crane's
Lost in a great overcoat of wings.

Soon out from my sight off went the big Meath man
Dodging the reeds of his nine-mile road.
So I lolled, as a bard bereft of his dæmon
Or a Moses awaiting a light-burdened cloud;
But heaven lay low all naked and brazen
Within the mad calm on that desert of green,
Where nothing, not even the water, is lean,
Where the orderly touches of Thought aren't seen –
And yet not a wild thought sang in my noddle;
Ah, how could it sing, while speed bit each heel,
While heat tugged a tight noose into my throttle
And while, on my spine, the hung head went nodding
As on it fierce light picked with a black bill.

Then where in soft Meath can one find ease?
When the sun, like a scare-crow, stands in those meadows
Guarding their glory, not even the breeze,
That ghostly rogue, can crop a shadow;
When even I asked for 'A drink, if you please,'
A woman, as proud as a motherly sow,
Hoked out of my way and hid where a larch
Leant like a derrick across an old barge
Stocked in the reeds; and so I went parched!
Ah, but soon down the Boyne, there, O the surprise
From a leaping fish – that silver flicker –
Was nothing compared to what hit my eyes:
An innocent house, marked 'Licensed for Liquor!'

Could anyone treat me to brighter green meadows
Than the Meath man who finished his thirsty plan when
Between every swig he mooned through those windows?
And yet, on my oath, it was easier then
To coop a mountainy cloud in a henhouse
Than to group the Meath light into lines for my pen;
And still I must bless him since beauty was caught

In ears that were drumming, in eyes all sweat,
In nostrils slimmed by indrawn breath;
For I made, as we lay in the grass by that road
This poem – a gem from the head of a toad;
So here, will you take it – hall-marked by a day
Over the hills and far away?

Brinsley was a great believer in ghosts, in a humorous sort
of a way, and he was, I often felt, a sibling of Jonathan Swift.
He wrote about his vision of the Dean.

ON SEEING SWIFT IN LARACOR

I saw them walk that lane again
And watch the midges cloud a pool,
Laughing at something in the brain –
The Dean and Patrick Brell the fool.

Like Lear he kept his fool with him
Long into Dublin's afterglow,
Until the wits in him grew dim
And Patrick sold him for a show.

Here were the days before Night came,
When Stella and the other – 'slut',
Vanessa, called by him – that flame
When Laracor was Lilliput!

And here, by walking up and down,
He made a man called Gulliver,
While bits of lads came out from town
To have a squint at him and her.

Still, was it Stella that they saw,
Or else some lassie of their own?
For in his story that's the flaw,
The secret no one since has known.

Was it some wench among the corn
Had set him from the other two,
Some tenderness that he had torn,
Some lovely blossom that he knew?

From Ulster to Leinster

For when Vanessa died of love,
And Stella learned to keep her place,
His Dublin soon the story wove
That steeped them in the Dean's disgrace.

They did not know, 'twas he could tell!
The reason of his wildest rages,
The story kept by Patrick Brell,
The thing that put him with the ages.

Now when they mention of the Dean
Some silence holds them as they talk;
Some things there are unsaid, unseen,
That drive me to this lonely walk,

To meet the mighty man again,
And yet no comfort comes to me.
Although sometimes I see him plain,
That silence holds the Hill of Bree.

For, though I think I'd know her well,
I've never seen her on his arm,
Laughing with him, nor heard her tell
She had forgiven all that harm.

And yet I'd like to know 'twere true,
That here at last in Laracor,
Here in the memory of a few,
There was this rest for him and her.

Still I am indebted to Donagh MacDonagh's anthology,
so I must pay his ghost the compliment of quoting another
of his poems – to be sung, he said, to the tune of 'The
Lowlands of Holland':

GOING TO MASS LAST SUNDAY

Going to Mass last Sunday my true love passed me by,
I knew her mind was altered by the rolling of her eye;
And when I stood in God's dark light my tongue could word no prayer
Knowing my saint had fled and left her reliquary bare.

109

Sweet faces smiled from holy glass, demure in saintly love,
Sweet voices ripe with Latin grace rolled from the choir above;
But brown eyes under Sunday wear were all my liturgy;
How can she hope for heaven who has so deluded me?

When daffodils were altar gold her lips were light on mine
And when the hawthorn flame was bright we drank the year's new wine;
The nights seemed stained-glass windows lit with love that paled the sky,
But love's last ember perishes in the winter of her eye.

Drape every downcast day now in purple cloth of Lent,
Smudge every forehead now with ash, that she may yet repent,
Who going to Mass last Sunday could pass so proudly by
And show her mind was altered by the rolling of an eye.

Thomas MacDonagh translated from the Irish of Cathal
Buidhe Mac Giolla Gunna (or Blondie Charley Gunn) the
immortal poem about the nature of love, poetry, drink, and
the thirsty, long-necked, yellow bittern:

THE YELLOW BITTERN

    The yellow bittern that never broke out
    In a drinking-bout, might as well have drunk;
    His bones are thrown on a naked stone
    Where he lived alone like a hermit monk.
    O yellow bittern! I pity your lot,
    Though they say that a sot like myself is curst –
    I was sober a while, but I'll drink and be wise
    For fear I should die in the end of thirst.

    It's not for the common birds that I'd mourn,
    The blackbird, the corncrake or the crane,
    But for the bittern that's shy and apart
    And drinks from the marsh from the lone bog-drain.
    Oh! if I had known you were near your death,
    While my breath held out I'd have run to you,
    Till a splash from the lake of the Son of the Bird
    Your soul would have stirred and waked anew.

    My darling told me to drink no more
    Or my life would be o'er in a little short while;

But I told her 'tis drink gives me health and strength,
And will lengthen my road by many a mile.
You see how the bird of the long smooth neck,
Could get his death from the thirst at last –
Come, son of my soul, and drain your cup,
You'll get no sup when your life is past.

In a wintering island by Constantine's halls,
A bittern calls from a wineless place,
And tells me that hither he cannot come
Till the summer is here and the sunny days.
When he crosses the stream there and wings o'er the sea,
Then a fear comes to me he may fail in his flight –
Well, the milk and the ale are drunk every drop,
And a dram won't stop our thirst this night.

We seem, at the moment, to be far away from Dublin. But Dublin is (is it not?) the centre of Ireland, and I can sit here at the centre, and, all around to the sea, survey and listen to the songs of my people.

F.R. Higgins, a notable public figure in my early days in Dublin, remembered with great affection his dear friend, Padraic Ó Conaire, storyteller and wandering man. And in Padraic's memory and honour, Higgins wrote the most moving elegy, which links Winetavern Street, in the heart of Old Dublin, with the ways of Wicklow, and the Spanish Arch in Galway, and with all the roads of Ireland. The best man to speak this poem is, as we all know, Sean Mac Réamoinn:

PADRAIC O'CONAIRE – GAELIC STORYTELLER

They've paid the last respects in sad tobacco
And silent is this wakehouse in its haze;
They've paid the last respects; and now their whiskey
Flings laughing words on mouths of prayer and praise;
And so young couples huddle by the gables,
O let them grope home through the hedgy night –
Alone I'll mourn my old friend, while the cold dawn
Thins out the holy candlelight.

111

Respects are paid to one loved by the people;
Ah, was he not – among our mighty poor –
The sudden wealth cast on those pools of darkness,
Those bearing, just, a star's faint signature;
And so he was to me, close friend, near brother,
Dear Padraic of the wide and sea-cold eyes –
So lovable, so courteous and noble,
The very West was in his soft replies.

They'll miss his heavy stick and stride in Wicklow –
His story-talking down Winetavern Street,
Where old men sitting in the wizen daylight
Have kept an edge upon his gentle wit;
While women on the grassy streets of Galway,
Who hearken for his passing – but in vain,
Shall hardly tell his step as shadows vanish
Through archways of forgotten Spain.

Ah, they'll say: Padraic's gone again exploring;
But now down glens of brightness, O he'll find
An alehouse overflowing with fine Gaelic
That's braced in vigour by the bardic mind,
And there his thoughts shall find their own forefathers –
In minds to whom our heights of race belong,
In crafty men, who ribbed a ship or turned
The secret joinery of song.

Alas, death mars the parchment of his forehead;
And yet for him, I know, the earth is mild –
The windy fidgets of September grasses
Can never tease a mind that loved the wild;
So drink his peace – this grey juice of the barley
Runs with a light that ever pleased his eye –
While old flames nod and gossip on the hearthstone
And only the young winds cry.

And now consider, and memorize, this brilliant note on
Georgian Dublin. The scholarly poet is Maurice Craig, who
has also written the final book on the matter and who is a
most learned, and unassuming, authority in many lands of
scholarship:

GEORGIAN DUBLIN

'So much to do,' said Turgot, 'and so little
Time to do it.' Civilisation must wait
Impotently crouching over the grate,
Watching to seize the moment, the boiling kettle;
Must grasp it suddenly, deftly, like a nettle,
Without reluctance, not too early or late,
That in the flawed alembic of the State
Correct precipitates may form and settle.
In the quick sunlight of those thirty years
This Roman Empire waited for Sedan,
Though now their building is a hollow shell,
That sea-worn tracery can move to tears.
This capital is incorruptible,
Doric, Ionic and Corinthian.

Like any city anywhere or, for that matter, any crossroads, Dublin has its ghosts. Ghosts are, after all, only memories. We all have loved the legend of Oliver Goldsmith, threadbare student in Trinity College, and not an over-zealous student, writing ballads and selling them for pence to street-singers. And then haunting the corners up in the Liberties to hear his own songs sung. His ghost may, perhaps, be encountered in Temple Bar, now restored to fashion and an abode for Trinity students.

That legend might, and certainly should, be true. None of the ballad, alas, has come down to us. But the man who wrote about the man and dog, the mad one, in Islington, London, may have been remembering and echoing earlier efforts. Anyway why should London have total claim to the piece? Men and mad dogs are the same the whole world over.

AN ELEGY ON THE DEATH OF A MAD DOG

Good people, all, of every sort,
Give ear unto my song;

And if you find it wond'rous short,
It cannot hold you long.

In Islington there was a man,
Of whom the world might say,
That still a godly race he ran,
Whene'er he went to pray.

A kind and gentle heart he had,
To comfort friends and foes;
The naked every day he clad,
When he put on his clothes.

And in that town a dog was found,
As many dogs there be,
Both mongrel, puppy, whelp, and hound,
And curs of low degree.

This dog and man at first were friends;
But when a pique began,
The dog, to gain some private ends,
Went mad and bit the man.

Around from all the neighbouring streets
The wond'ring neighbours ran,
And swore the dog had lost his wits,
To bite so good a man.

The wound it seemed both sore and sad
To every Christian eye;
And while they swore the dog was mad,
They swore the man would die.

But soon a wonder came to light,
That shew'd the rogues they lied:
The man recover'd of the bite,
The dog it was that died.

Which of us has not met, at least once, the ghost of James
Clarence Mangan, up the slope there in Summerhill or in a
shady corner of Mountjoy Square. Several times I have
spoken to him. Or he to me.

He died young and had little or no sense of the passage of time and, after a suggestion from another poet from faraway places, he seemed to think that twenty years was a long time. It all depends on where and how you spend them.

But not really long, I say to him, when you have staggered as far as seventy-two.

But let him speak for himself as most movingly he did:

TWENTY GOLDEN YEARS AGO

O, the rain, the weary, dreary rain,
How it plashes on the window-sill!
Night, I guess too, must be on the wane,
Strass and gass around are grown so still.
Here I sit, with coffee in my cup –
Ah! 'twas rarely I beheld it flow
In the tavern where I loved to sup
Twenty golden years ago!

Twenty years ago, alas! – but stay –
On my life, 'tis half-past twelve o'clock!
After all, the hours do slip away –
Come, here goes to burn another block!
For the night, or morn, is wet and cold;
And my fire is dwindling rather low: –
I had fire enough, when young and bold
Twenty golden years ago.

Dear! I don't feel well at all, somehow:
Few in Weimar dream how bad I am;
Floods of tears grow common with me now,
High-Dutch floods, that Reason cannot dam.
Doctors think I'll neither live nor thrive
If I mope at home so – I don't know –
Am I living now? I was alive
Twenty golden years ago.

Wifeless, friendless, flagonless, alone,
Not quite bookless, though, unless I choose,
Left with nought to do, except to groan,

And as I Rode by Granard Moat

Not a soul to woo, except the muse –
O! this is hard for me to bear,
Me, who whilome lived so much en haut,
Me, who broke all hearts like china-ware,
Twenty golden years ago!

Perhaps, 'tis better; – time's defacing waves
Long have quenched the radiance of my brow –
They who curse me nightly from their graves,
Scarce could love me were they living now;
But my loneliness hath darker ills –
Such dull duns as Conscience, Thought and Co.,
Awful Gorgons! worse than tailors' bills
Twenty golden years ago!

Did I paint a fifth of what I feel,
O, how plaintive you would ween I was!
But I won't, albeit I have a deal
More to wail about than Kerner has!
Kerner's tears are kept for withered flowers,
Mine for withered hopes, my scroll of woe
Dates, alas! from youth's deserted bowers,
Twenty golden years ago!
Yet, may Deutschland's bardlings flourish long,
Me, I tweak no beak among them; – hawks
Must not pounce on hawks: besides, in song
I could once beat all of them by chalks.
Though you find me as I near my goal,
Sentimentalizing like Rousseau,
O! I had a grand Byronian soul
Twenty golden years ago!

Tick-tick, tick-tick! – not a sound save Time's,
And the windgust as it drives the rain –
Tortured torturer of reluctant rhymes,
Go to bed, and rest thine aching brain!
Sleep! – no more the dupe of hopes or schemes;
Soon thou sleepest where the thistles blow –
Curious anticlimax to thy dreams
Twenty golden years ago!

And lifting his eyes and his imagination from the poverties and miseries of his life in Dublin, Mangan, with the aid of an ancient Persian poet, looked back to the days of a notable dynasty. Which goes to show that from Dublin, on a clear day and with a clear mind, you can see the world, present and past and, perhaps, to come:

THE TIME OF THE BARMECIDES

My eyes are filmed, my beard is grey,
I am bowed with the weight of years;
I would I were stretched in my bed of clay,
With my long-lost youth's compeers!
For back to the Past, though the thought brings woe,
My memory ever glides –
To the old, old time, long, long ago,
The time of the Barmecides!
To the old, old time, long, long ago,
The time of the Barmecides.

Then Youth was mine, and a fierce wild will,
And an iron arm in war,
And a fleet foot high upon Ishkar's hill,
When the watch-light glimmered afar,
And a barb as fiery as any I know
That Khoord or Beddaween rides,
Ere my friends lay low – long, long ago,
In the time of the Barmecides,
Ere my friends lay low – long, long ago,
In the time of the Barmecides.

One golden goblet illumed my board,
One silver dish was there;
At hand my tried Karamanian sword
Lay always bright and bare,
For those were the days when the angry blow
Supplanted the word that chides –
When hearts could glow – long, long ago,
In the time of the Barmecides,
When hearts could glow – long, long ago,
In the time of the Barmecides.

Through city and desert my mates and I
Were free to rove and roam,
Our diapered canopy the deep of the sky,
Or the roof of the palace-dome –
Oh! ours was that vivid life to and fro
Which only sloth derides: –
Men spent Life so, long, long ago,
In the time of the Barmecides,
Men spent Life so, long, long ago,
In the time of the Barmecides.

I see rich Baghdad once again,
With its turrets of Moorish mould,
And the Khalif's twice five hundred men
Whose binishes flamed with gold;
I call up many a gorgeous show
Which the Pall of Oblivion hides –
All passed like snow, long, long ago,
With the time of the Barmecides;
All passed like snow, long, long ago,
With the time of the Barmecides!

But mine eye is dim, and my beard is gray,
And I bend with the weight of years –
May I soon go down to the House of Clay
Where slumber my Youth's compeers!
For with them and the Past, though the thought wakes woe,
My memory ever abides,
And I mourn for the Times gone long ago,
For the Times of the Barmecides!
I mourn for the Times gone long ago,
For the Times of the Barmecides!

But much closer to Dublin, and from the seventeenth-century Irish, Mangan re-echoed that imperishable poem, and song, about the proud and wealthy woman: 'The Woman of Three Cows'. Once upon a time I asked the great Colm Ó Lochlainn to what tune this could be sung. He said (I forget what the year was) that I was listening to the tune every day on the radio and the words that went with it were about Ghost Riders in the Sky. But the original was, he told me, a dance-tune called 'My Love is in America'.

And thus, as Tennyson hinted, the whole round earth is, every way, bound by gold chains about the feet of God.

Anyway, go ahead and sing:

O Woman of Three Cows, a-gradh! don't let your tongue thus rattle!
O don't be saucy, don't be stiff, because you may have cattle,
I have seen – and, here's my hand to you, I only say what's true –
A many a one with twice your stock not half so proud as you.

Good luck to you, don't scorn the poor, and don't be their despiser;
For worldly wealth soon melts away, and cheats the very miser:
And death soon strips the proudest wreath from haughty human brows,
Then don't be stiff, and don't be proud, good Woman of Three Cows!

See where Momonia's heroes lie, proud Owen More's descendants,
'Tis they that won the glorious name, and had the grand attendants,
If they were forced to bow to Fate, as every mortal bows,
Can you be proud, can you be stiff, my Woman of Three Cows?

The brave sons of the Lords of Clare, they left the land to mourning;
Mo bhrón! for they were banished, with no hope of their returning –
Who knows in what abodes of want those youths were driven to house?
Yet you can give yourself these airs, O Woman of Three Cows!

Think of O'Donnell of the ships, the Chief whom nothing daunted –
See how he fell in distant Spain, unchronicled, unchanted!
He sleeps, the great O'Sullivan, where thunder cannot rouse –
Then ask yourself, should you be proud, good Woman of Three Cows!

O'Ruark, Maguire, those souls of fire, whose names are shrined in story –
Think how their high achievements once made Erin's greatest glory –
Yet now their bones lie mouldering under weeds and cypress boughs,
And so, for all your pride, will yours, O Woman of Three Cows!

The O'Carrolls, also, famed when fame was only for the boldest,
Rest in forgotten sepulchres with Erin's best and oldest;
Yet who so great as they of yore in battle or carouse?
Just think of that, and hide your head, good Woman of Three Cows!

Your neighbour's poor, and you, it sems, are big with vain ideas,
Because, an eadh! you've got three cows, one more, I see, than she has;
That tongue of yours wags more at times than charity allows –
But, if you're strong, be merciful, great Woman of Three Cows!

Now, there you go! You still, of course, keep up your scornful bearing,
And I'm too poor to hinder you; but, by the cloak I'm wearing,
If I had but four cows myself, even though you were my spouse,
I'd thwack you well to cure your pride, my Woman of Three Cows!

Far, far away from the proud woman and her thundering
herds was the poet when he looked to the East and
meditated on mortality and the vanity of all human ambition
and, from the streets of Dublin, asked some hard questions
of King Solomon:

GONE IN THE WIND

Solomon! where is thy throne? It is gone in the wind.
Babylon! where is thy might? It is gone in the wind.
Like the swift shadows of Noon, like the dreams of the Blind,
Vanish the glories and pomp of the earth in the wind.

Man! canst thou build upon aught in the pride of thy mind?
Wisdom will teach thee that nothing can tarry behind;
Though there be thousand bright actions embalmed and enshrined,
Myriads and millions of brighter are snow in the wind.

Solomon! where is thy throne? It is gone in the wind.
Babylon! where is thy might? It is gone in the wind.
All that the genius of man hath achieved or designed
Waits but its hour to be dealt with as dust by the wind.

Say, what is Pleasure? A phantom, a mask undefined.
Science? An almond, whereof we can pierce but the rind.
Honour and Affluence? Firmans that Fortune hath signed
Only to glitter and pass on the wings of the wind.

Solomon! where is thy throne? It is gone in the wind.
Babylon! Where is thy might? It is gone in the wind.
Who is the Fortunate? He who in anguish hath pined!
He shall rejoice when his relics are dust in the wind!

Moral! be careful with what thy best hopes are entwined;
Woe to the miners for Truth – where the Lampless have mined!
Woe to the seekers on earth for – what none ever find!
They and their trust shall be scattered like leaves on the wind.

Solomon! where is thy throne? It is gone in the wind.
Babylon! Where is thy might? It is gone in the wind.
Happy in death they only whose hearts have consigned
All Earth's affections and longings and cares to the wind.

Pity, thou, reader! the madness of poor Humankind,
Raving of Knowledge, – and Satan so busy to blind!
Raving of Glory, – like me, – for the garlands I bind
(Garlands of song) are but gathered, and – strewn in the wind!

Solomon! where is thy throne? It is gone in the wind.
Babylon! Where is thy might? It is gone in the wind.
I, Abul-Namez, must rest, for my fire hath declined,
And I hear voices from Hades like bells on the wind!

If you are looking for ghosts in the neighbourhood of
Dublin you must encounter first of all, and with all due
respects to Saint Patrick and King Sitric, that shrewd invader
from Limerick, Brian Boru or Brían na Boroimhe, of the
Tributes.

It has happened to me that I was not barred but excom-
municated from a certain licensed premises in Donnybrook
for proclaiming in a loud voice, and in a heated argument
with some learned colleagues, that Brian of the Tributes was
a tax-collector from Limerick and that the Danes were
decent men trying to do something practical: and that, in
the end, one of them was driven to hitting him with a
hatchet, when he was supposed to be saying his prayers.

May his saintly ghost, and the outraged publican, forgive
me.

And here let Brian speak for himself as William Kennelly
heard him speaking before the ruckus at Clontarf.

And as I Rode by Granard Moat

Stand ye now for Erin's glory! Stand ye now for Erin's cause!
Long ye've groaned beneath the rigour of the Northmen's savage laws.
What, though brothers league against us? What, though myriads be the
　　foe?
Victory will be more honoured in the myriads' overthrow.

Proud Connacians! oft we've wrangled, in our petty feuds of yore;
Now we fight against the robber Dane, upon our native shore;
May our hearts unite in friendship, as our blood in one red tide,
While we crush their mail-clad legions, and annihilate their pride!

Brave Eugenians! Erin triumphs in the sight she sees today –
Desmond's homesteads all deserted for the muster and the fray!
Cluan's vale and Galtee's summit send their bravest and their best –
May such hearts be theirs forever, for the Freedom of the West!

Chiefs and Kerne of Dalcassia! Brothers of my past career,
Oft we've trodden on the pirate-flag that flaunts below us here,
You remember Iniscattery, how we bounded on the foe,
As the torrent of the mountain bursts upon the plain below!

They have razed our proudest castles – spoiled the Temples of the Lord –
Burnt to dust the sacred relics – put the Peaceful to the sword –
Desecrated all things holy – as they soon may do again,
If their power to-day we smite not – if to-day we be not men!

Slaughtered pilgrims is the story at St Kevin's rocky cell,
And on the southern sea-shore, at Isle Helig's holy well;
E'en the anchorets are hunted, poor and peaceful though they be,
And not one of them left living, in their caves beside the sea!

Think of all your murder'd chieftains – all your rifled homes and shrines –
Then rush down, with whetted vengeance, like fierce wolves upon their
　　lines!
Think of Bangor – think of Mayo – and Senanus' holy tomb –
Think of all your past endurance – what may be your future doom!

On this day the God-man suffered, look upon the sacred sign –
May we conquer 'neath its shadow, as of old did Constantine!
May the heathen tribes of Odin fade before it like a dream,
And the triumph of this glorious day in future annals gleam!

From Ulster to Leinster

God of Heaven, bless our banner – nerve our sinews for the strife!
Fight we now for all that's holy – for our altars, land, and life –
For red vengeance on the spoiler, whom the blazing temples trace –
For the honour of our maidens, and the glory of our race!

Should I fall before the foeman, 'tis the death I seek to-day;
Should ten thousand daggers pierce me, bear my body not away,
Till this day of days be over – till the field is fought and won –
Then the holy Mass be chaunted, and the funeral rites be done.

Curses darker than Ben Heder light upon the craven slave
Who prefers the life of traitor to the glory of the grave!
Freedom's guerdon now awaits you, or a destiny of chains –
Trample down the dark oppressor while one spark of life remains!

Think not now of coward mercy – Heaven's curse is on their blood!
Spare them not, though myriad corpses float upon the purple flood!
By the memory of great Daithi, and the valiant chiefs of yore,
This day we'll scourge the viper brood for ever from our shore!

Men of Erin! men of Erin! grasp the battle-axe and spear!
Chase these Northern wolves before you like a herd of frightened deer!
Burst their ranks, like bolts from heaven! Down on the heathen crew,
For the glory of the Crucifix, and Erin's glory too!

Perhaps the most notable of Dublin's ghosts answers, if you call him, to the name of James Joyce. Not only does he continue to walk the streets by night and day and, every Bloomsday, to manifest himself to more and more people. But, like the Lord Himself, he created other people, whose ghosts also parade most impressively: Stephen Dedalus, for instance, whose ghost is a shadow of his Maker.

I feel that Joyce, in his time, must have considered this poem in which the German John Sterling, in 1840, lamented the epic aerial passing of that enchanting figure from Greek legend:

LAMENT FOR DÆDALUS

Wail for Dædalus, all that is fairest!
All that is tuneful in air or wave!

And as I Rode by Granard Moat

Shapes whose beauty is truest and rarest,
Haunt with your lamps and spells his grave!

Statues, bend your heads in sorrow,
Ye that glance 'mid ruins old,
That know not a past, nor expect a morrow
On many a moonlight Grecian wold!

By sculptur'd cave and darken'd river
Thee, Dædalus, oft the nymphs recall;
The leaves with a sound of winter quiver,
Murmur thy name, and withering fall.

Yet are thy visions in soul the grandest
Of all that crowd on the tear-dimm'd eye,
Though, Dædalus, thou no more commandest
New stars to that ever-widening sky.

Ever thy phantoms arise before us,
Our loftier brothers, but one in blood;
By bed and table they lord it o'er us
With looks of beauty and words of good.

They tell us and show us of man victorious
O'er all that's blameless, blind, and base;
Their presence has made our nature glorious,
And given our night an illumined face.

Thy toil has won them a godlike quiet;
Thou hast wrought their path to a lovely sphere;
Their eyes to calm rebuke our riot,
And shape us a home of refuge here.

For Dædalus breathed in them his spirit;
In them their sire his beauty sees:
We too, a younger brood, inherit
The gifts and blessing bestow'd on these.

But, ah! their wise and bounteous seeming
Recalls the more that the sage is gone;
Weeping we wake from deceitful dreaming,
And find our voiceless chamber lone.

Dædalus, thou from the twilight fleest,
Which thou with visions hast made so bright;

And when no more those shapes thou seest,
Wanting thine eye they lose their light.

Ev'n in the noblest of man's creations,
Those fresh worlds round those old of ours,
When the seer is gone, the orphan'd nations
Know but the tombs of perish'd Powers.

Wail for Dædalus, Earth and Ocean!
Stars and Sun, lament for him!
Ages, quake in strange commotion!
All ye realms of life, be dim!

Wail for Dædalus, awful voices,
From earth's deep centre mankind appal;
Seldom ye sound, and then Death rejoices,
For he knows that then the mightiest fall.

The wonderful Oliver St John Gogarty is the first man mentioned, under another name, in that long book, a novel or something, by James Joyce. But no man could ever dare to say that Dr Gogarty was a ghost.

He had a deep devotion to swans. He had some trouble once with some gentlemen carrying guns who did not approve of his variety of politics. He abandoned the argument and withdrew from their company by jumping into and swimming the Liffey. And always afterwards he felt indebted to the river and the swans thereon. He even donated more swans to the balustraded stream. But, better still, he paid his respects, in his 'Leda and the Swan', to one of the earliest and greatest stories about the bird:

Though her mother told her
Not to go a-bathing,
Leda loved the river
And she could not keep away:
Wading in its freshets
When the noon was heavy;
Walking by the water
At the close of day.

And as I Rode by Granard Moat

Where beneath its waterfalls,
Underneath the beeches,
Gently flows a broader
Hardly moving stream,
And the balanced trout lie
In the quiet reaches;
Taking all her clothes off,
Leda went to swim.

There was not a flag-leaf
By the river's margin
That might be a shelter
From a passer-by;
And a sudden whiteness
In the quiet darkness,
Let alone the splashing,
Was enough to catch an eye.

But the place was lonely,
And her clothes were hidden;
Even cattle walking
In the ford had gone away;
Every single farm-hand
Sleeping after dinner, –
What's the use of talking?
There was no one in the way.

In, without a stitch on,
Peaty water yielded,
Till her head was lifted
With its ropes of hair;
It was more surprising
Than a lily gilded,
Just to see how golden
Was her body there:

Lolling in the water,
Lazily uplifting
Limbs that on the surface
Whitened into snow;
Leaning on the water,
Indolently drifting,

From Ulster to Leinster

Hardly any faster
Than the foamy bubbles go.

You would say to see her
Swimming in the lonely
Pool, or after, dryer,
Putting on her clothes:
'O but she is lovely,
Not a soul to see her,
And how lovely only
Leda's Mother knows!'

Under moving branches
Leisurely she dresses,
And the leafy sunlight
Made you wonder were
All its woven shadows
But her golden tresses,
Or a smock of sunlight
For her body bare.

When on earth great beauty
Goes exempt from danger,
It will be endangered
From a source on high;
When unearthly stillnes
Falls on leaves, the ranger,
In his wood-lore anxious,
Gazes at the sky.

While her hair was drying,
Came a gentle languor,
Whether from the bathing
Or the breeze she didn't know.
Anyway she lay there,
And her Mother's anger
(Worse if she had wet hair)
Could not make her dress and go.

Whitest of all earthly
Things, the white that's rarest,
Is the snow on mountains

And as I Rode by Granard Moat

Standing in the sun;
Next the clouds above them,
Then the down is fairest
On the breast and pinions
Of a proudly sailing swan.

And she saw him sailing
On the pool where lately
She had stretched unnoticed,
As she thought, and swum;
And she never wondered
Why, erect and stately,
Where no river weed was
Such a bird had come.

What was it she called him:
Gosey-goosey gander?
For she knew no better
Way to call a swan;
And the bird responding
Seemed to understand her,
For he left his sailing
For the bank to waddle on.

Apple blossoms under
Hills of Lacedaemon,
With the snow beyond them
In the still blue air,
To the swans who hid them
With his wings asunder,
Than the breasts of Leda,
Were not lovelier!

Of the tales that daughters
Tell their poor old mothers,
Which by all accounts are
Often very odd;
Leda's was a story
Stranger than all others.
What was there to say but:
Glory be to God?

And she half-believed her,
For she knew her daughter;
And she saw the swan-down
Tangled in her hair.
Though she knew how deeply
Runs the stillest water;
How could she protect her
From the winged air?

Why is it effects are
Greater than their causes?
Why should causes often
Differ from effects?
Why should what is lovely
Fill the world with harness?
And the most deceived be
She who least suspects?

When the hyacinthine
Eggs were in the basket,
Blue as at the whiteness
Where a cloud begins:
Who would dream there lay there
All that Trojan brightness;
Agamemnon murdered;
And the mighty Twins?

Patrick Kavanagh is still a living voice in Dublin and, by the hand of the sculptor John Coll, he sits contemplating the waters of his beloved Grand Canal, remembering what he thought when he walked along the disused towing-path:

CANAL BANK WALK

Leafy-with-love banks and the green waters of the canal
Pouring redemption for me, that I do
The will of God, wallow in the habitual, the banal,
Grow with nature again as before I grew.
The bright stick trapped, the breeze adding a third
Party to the couple kissing on an old seat,
And a bird gathering materials for the nest for the Word

Eloquently new and abandoned to its delirious beat.
O unworn world enrapture me, encapture me in a web
Of fabulous grass and eternal voices by a beech,
Feed the gaping need of my senses, give me ad lib
To pray unselfconsciously with overflowing speech
For this soul needs to be honoured with a new dress woven
From green and blue things and arguments that cannot be proven.

One seat on the canal bank was erected in memory of Mrs Dermot O'Brien, the wife of a great painter. That seat, because of the dedication and artistic associations, meant a great deal to Kavanagh, and set him to wishing that he might be similarly remembered. And thanks to John Ryan, and others who followed his lead, his wish was fulfilled.

LINES WRITTEN ON A SEAT ON THE GRAND CANAL

O commemorate me where there is water,
Canal water preferably, so stilly
Greeny at the heart of summer. Brother
Commemorate me thus beautifully.
Where by a lock Niagorously roars
The falls for those who sit in the tremendous silence
Of mid-July. No one will speak in prose
Who finds his way to these Parnassian islands.
A swan goes by head low with many apologies,
Fantastic light looks through the eyes of bridges –
And look! A barge comes bringing from Athy
And other far-flung towns mythologies.
O commemorate me with no hero-courageous
Tomb – just a canal-bank seat for the passer-by.

And was it walking by the bank of that canal and hearing the music of the wind in the topmost branches of the trees, that the poet Austin Clarke found himself far away by miles but much farther by centuries – and became the monk of ancient times who was enchanted for an instant, or an eternity, out of this earth when he hearkened to the singing of 'The Blackbird of Derrycairn'?

Stop, stop and listen for the bough top
Is whistling and the sun is brighter
Than God's own shadow in the cup now!
Forget the hour-bell. Mournful matins
Will sound, Patric, as well at nightfall.

Faintly through mist of broken water
Fionn heard my melody in Norway.
He found the forest track, he brought back
This beak to gild the branch and tell, there,
Why men must welcome in the daylight.

He loved the breeze that warns the black grouse,
The shouts of gillies in the morning
When packs are counted and the swans cloud
Loch Erne, but more than all those voices
My throat rejoicing from the hawthorn.

In little cells behind a cashel,
Patric, no handbell gives a glad sound.
But knowledge is found among the branches.
Listen! The song that shakes my feathers
Will thong the leather of your satchels.

Once upon a time (and that's the proper opening for this
story) I was chosen, and honoured to be chosen, to travel in
the back of a taxi all the way from Dublin Airport to the far
southern boundary of Dublin city, in the company of a
beautiful American film-actress. The man who did the
choosing was Ernie Anderson, right-hand man to John
Huston.

The idea was that I was to act as the beautiful lady's guide
to Dublin, ancient and modern, and I set out to do my best.
I discovered that the lady knew, all things considered, as
much as I did. She was well read and/or well briefed by the
inimitable Ernie.

And I was mute in wonder and admiration when, as we
were passing the General Post Office, she started to recite
the sonorous and solemn words of Patrick Pearse:

And as I Rode by Granard Moat

THE FOOL

Since the wise men have not spoken, I speak that am only a fool;
A fool that hath loved his folly,
Yea, more than the wise men their books or their counting houses, or
    their quiet homes,
Or their fame in men's mouths;
A fool that in all his days hath done never a prudent thing,
Never hath counted the cost, nor recked if another reaped
The fruit of his mighty sowing, content to scatter the seed;
A fool that is unrepentant, and that soon at the end of all
Shall laugh in his lonely heart as the ripe ears fall to the reaping-hooks
And the poor are filled that were empty,
Tho' he go hungry.

I have squandered the splendid years that the Lord God gave to my youth
In attempting impossible things, deeming them alone worth the toil.
Was it folly or grace? Not men shall judge me, but God.
I have squandered the splendid years:
Lord, if I had the years I would squander them over again,
Aye, fling them from me!
For this I have heard in my heart, that a man shall scatter, not hoard,
Shall do the deed of to-day, nor take thought of to-morrow's teen,
Shall not bargain or huxter with God; or was it a jest of Christ's
And is this my sin before men, to have taken Him at His word?

The lawyers have sat in council, the men with the keen, long faces,
And said, 'This man is a fool,' and others have said, 'He blasphemeth';
And the wise have pitied the fool that hath striven to give a life
In the world of time and space among the bulks of actual things,
To a dream that was dreamed in the heart, and that only the heart could
    hold.

O wise men, riddle me this: what if the dream come true?
What if the dream come true? and if millions unborn shall dwell
In the house that I shaped in my heart, the noble house of my thought?
Lord, I have staked my soul, I have staked the lives of my kin
On the truth of Thy dreadful word. Do not remember my failures,
But remember this my faith.

And so I speak.
Yea, ere my hot youth pass, I speak to my people and say:

Ye shall be foolish as I; ye shall scatter, not save;
Ye shall venture your all, lest ye lose what is more than all;
Ye shall call for a miracle, taking Christ at His word.
And for this I will answer, O people, answer here and hereafter,
O people that I have loved, shall we not answer together?

At a later date in our brief acquaintance that lovely lady suggested, at a party of friends in Dalkey, that I should read out aloud the prayer that Mr Yeats prayed for his daughter. The lady said: 'You have daughters. And a deep voice. Mr Yeats had a deep voice. I was a daughter. And any man who ever had a daughter should have ambitioned to write such a prayer for his daughter. And any daughter would admire to have such a prayer prayed for her. So read.'

So, to the best of my ability and in all humility, I read:

A PRAYER FOR MY DAUGHTER

Once more the storm is howling, and half hid
Under this cradle-hood and coverlid
My child sleeps on. There is no obstacle
But Gregory's wood and one bare hill
Whereby the haystack- and roof-levelling wind,
Bred on the Atlantic, can be stayed;
And for an hour I have walked and prayed
Because of the great gloom that is in my mind.

I have walked and prayed for this young child an hour
And heard the sea-wind scream upon the tower,
And under the arches of the bridge, and scream
In the elms above the flooded stream;
Imagining in excited reverie
That the future years had come,
Dancing to a frenzied drum,
Out of the murderous innocence of the sea.

May she be granted beauty and yet not
Beauty to make a stranger's eye distraught,
Or hers before a looking-glass, for such,
Being made beautiful overmuch,

And as I Rode by Granard Moat

Consider beauty a sufficient end,
Lose natural kindness and maybe
The heart-revealing intimacy
That chooses right, and never find a friend.

Helen being chosen found life flat and dull
And later had much trouble from a fool,
While that great Queen, that rose out of the spray,
Being fatherless could have her way
Yet chose a bandy-leggèd smith for man.
It's certain that fine women eat
A crazy salad with their meat
Whereby the Horn of Plenty is undone.

In courtesy I'd have her chiefly learned;
Hearts are not had as a gift but hearts are earned
By those that are not entirely beautiful;
Yet many, that have played the fool
For beauty's very self, has charm made wise,
And many a poor man that has roved,
Loved and thought himself beloved,
From a glad kindness cannot take his eyes.

May she become a flourishing hidden tree
That all her thoughts may like the linnet be,
And have no business but dispensing round
Their magnanimities of sound,
Nor but in merriment begin a chase,
Nor but in merriment a quarrel.
O may she live like some green laurel
Rooted in one dear perpetual place.

My mind, because the minds that I have loved,
The sort of beauty that I have approved,
Prosper but little, has dried up of late,
Yet knows that to be choked with hate
May well be of all evil chances chief.
If there's no hatred in a mind
Assault and battery of the wind
Can never tear the linnet from the leaf.

An intellectual hatred is the worst,
So let her think opinions are accursed.
Have I not seen the loveliest woman born

Out of the mouth of Plenty's horn,
Because of her opinionated mind
Barter that horn and every good
By quiet natures understood
For an old bellows full of angry wind?

Considering that, all hatred driven hence,
The soul recovers radical innocence
And learns at last that it is self-delighting,
Self-appeasing, self-affrighting,
And that its own sweet will is Heaven's will;
She can, though every face should scowl
And every windy quarter howl
Or every bellows burst, be happy still.

And may her bridegroom bring her to a house
Where all's accustomed, ceremonious;
For arrogance and hatred are the wares
Peddled in the thoroughfares.
How but in custom and in ceremony
Are innocence and beauty born?
Ceremony's a name for the rich horn,
And custom for the spreading laurel tree.

That brought me a long way from Dalkey and Dublin. All the way to Ballylee and the Tower. But it sets me to thinking that poetry, born under a dancing star, can like Ariel go anywhere and girdle the earth in an instant.

The original Spanish lady, in balladry and the Irish popular mind, must have walked the streets of Galway city. But when Joseph Campbell, up from Antrim, met her, she was, he says, and we must believe him, walking in Dublin:

As I walked down through Dublin City
At the hour of twelve in the night,
Who should I spy but a Spanish Lady,
Washing her feet by candlelight?
First she dipped them, and then she dried them,
Over a fire of ambery coal.
Never in all my life did I see
A maid so neat about the sole.

And as I Rode by Granard Moat

I stopped to peep, but the Watchman passed,
And says: Young fellow, the night is late.
Get home to bed, or I'll wrastle you
At a double trot through the Bridewell gate!
So I waved a kiss to the Spanish Lady,
Hot as the fire of cramesy coal.
I've seen dark maids, though never one
So white and neat about the sole.

O, she's too rich for a Poddle swaddy,
With her tortoise comb and mantle fine.
A Hellfire buck would fit her better,
Drinking brandy and claret wine.
I'm just a decent College sizar,
Poor as a sod of smouldery coal;
And how would I dress the Spanish Lady,
And she so neat about the sole?

O, she'd make a mott for the Provost Marshal,
Or a wife for the Mayor on his coach so high,
Or a queen of Andalusia,
Kicking her heel in the Cardinal's eye.
I'm blue as cockles, brown as herrings
Over a grid of glimmery coal,
And all because of the Spanish Lady,
So mortial neat about the sole.

I wandered north, and I wandered south,
By Golden Lane and Patrick's Close,
The Coombe, Smithfield and Stoneybatter,
Back to Napper Tandy's house.
Old age has laid its hand upon me,
Cold as a fire of ashy coal. –
And where is the lovely Spanish Lady,
That maid so neat about the sole?

And it was in Dublin city, in the autumn of 1939, and in the home of Brian O'Higgins (Brian na Banban) in Hollybrook Road, Clontarf, that I first met, and began a most memorable friendship with, a lovely silver-haired lady, Teresa Brayton. And the following spring I was privileged to walk with her and with William Walsh, the elder brother of Michael Walsh, the poet of Fore, and with Brian O'Higgins of the Abbey Theatre, son of Brian na Banban, along the Old Bog Road about which she had written the famous song. You will find that road off the main road betwen Kilcock and Enfield. And on our own first meeting I was honoured to be able to quote to her, word-perfect I hope, another poem of hers that like 'The Old Bog Road' came out of the longing of the exile for the island home:

THE OLD ROAD HOME

I would know it in the darkness were I deaf and dumb and blind,
I would know it o'er the thrashing of a million miles of foam,
I would know it sun or shadow, I would know it rain or wind,
The road that leads to Ireland, aye, the old road home.

Sure the angels up in Heaven would be pointing it to me
From every track that man has made since first he learned to roam,
And my feet would leap to greet it like a captive thing set free
The road that leads to Ireland, aye, the old road home.

I would find the hawthorn bushes, I would find the boreen's gap
With one old cabin standing 'mid the soft and greening loam,
If the world was all a jumble on the great Creator's lap
I would know the road to Ireland, aye, the old road home.

And now that Teresa has brought us on our way, and for a while, to the soft and green Midlands, we may brood for a moment over that young man from the Boyne Valley, whose life, like that of a million or more others, was wasted on far and horrible foreign fields.

Francis Ledwidge here mourns lost loves and the many dead and, in a gentle poem, remembers his mother:

THE LOST ONES

Somewhere is music from the linnets' bills,
And thro' the sunny flowers the bee-wings drone,

And as I Rode by Granard Moat

And white bells of convolvulus on hills
Of quiet May make silent ringing, blown
Hither and thither by the wind of showers,
And somewhere all the wandering birds have flown;
And the brown breath of Autumn chills the flowers.

But where are all the loves of long ago?
Oh, little twilight ship blown up the tide,
Where are the faces laughing in the glow
Of morning years, the lost ones scattered wide?
Give me your hand, Oh brother, let us go
Crying about the dark for those who died.

MY MOTHER

God made my mother on an April day,
From sorrow and the mist along the sea,
Lost birds' and wanderers' songs and ocean spray,
And the moon loved her wandering jealously.

Beside the ocean's din she combed her hair,
Singing the nocturne of the passing ships,
Before her earthly lover found her there
And kissed away the music from her lips.

She came unto the hills and saw the change
That brings the swallow and the geese in turns,
But there was not a grief she deemed strange,
For there is that in her which always mourns.

Kind heart she has for all on hill or wave
Whose hopes grow wings like ants to fly away.
I bless the God who such a mother gave
This poor bird-hearted singer of a day.

III

From Leinster to Connacht

Well, Francis Ledwidge has brought us to the beautiful village of Slane, on the Boyne, and from the top of the Hill of Slane you may survey all Ireland.

Do I hear you say that I exaggerate? Well, perhaps in a physical sense, if you are thinking of altitudes above sea-level, contours, cloud-densities, et cetera. But in a spiritual sense?

St Patrick must have known something when he lighted his Paschal fire on the Hill of Slane and started something that, it was said, was never to die in Ireland (cynics have remarked that he was a bit of an optimist), and who are we to contradict a saint?

And from the top of the Hill of Slane I look to the north-west, or thereabouts, and see Collooney in the County Sligo. And I remember some of the lines about the Collooney boys who found themslves, it was said, in Gehenna:

> 'A dreadful dream I fain would tell.
> I dreamed I died and went to Hell.
> And there, upon the topmost landing,
> Some prime Collooney boys were standing.
> 'Then gazing round I wondered where
> Dwelt the scamps from Ballysodare,
>
> And musing thus, I scanned each face,
> And from within that dreadful place,
> Prisoners of every nationality
> And chaps renowned for all rascality,

My quest was vain. They were not there,
The rowdy rakes of Ballysodare.

"'Sir Nick," quoth I, "on every hand
I see your spoils from every land.
No doubt they well deserve their fate,
Their sins I wouldn't dare deflate,
But, might I ask you, is it fair
To quite pass over Ballysodare?"

"'Ha, Ha," quoth Nick, with sinister mirth,
"There's not a place on all this earth
Exempt from my bold operations,
Resist, who can, my machinations.
I'll take you lower still, and there
You'll find the bucks from Ballysodare."

'Still down we went to lower regions,
Encompassed by perspiring legions
From Straid, Kilvarnet and Killoran,
As well as Sligo and Bundoran.
Gaunt faces wore a look of worry,
Contingents, those, from Tobercurry.

'At length we reached a dungeon rude
In Limbo's lowest latitude,
And there I saw with apprehension
A saucepan grim, of vast dimension,
Upon a roaring furnace boiling
While stoking imps around were toiling.

'With conscious pride Old Nick drew near
The huge Utensil. In the rear,
I peered with horror o'er his shoulder.
Despite the heat my blood ran colder.
He raised the lid and said: "In there
I boil the boys from Ballysodare."'

Now that was an odd vision to see from the summit of St
Patrick's Slane. Whoever wrote that evil piece ... well, we
can only think, in mercy and charity towards him, that
something must have happened to him in Ballysodare. A

native of Ballysodare might rightfully say that whatever it was happened to him, he didn't get half enough.

But what about the involvement of the Collooney boys in that Dantean ballad?

Thirty years ago I talked about that business with Philip Rooney, author of *Captain Boycott*, *North Road*, *Singing River* and other novels. Philip was a gentleman of the first order who did me the honour of his friendship. He was also a Collooney boy. And Philip explained to me:

'Now the brawny men from North Galway and Mayo, on their way to Scotland in the old days for the potato harvest, took the Limerick to Collooney line, debarked at the station and walked across the town to embark at the Northern Counties station to continue their journey. So their tickets were always stamped "To Collooney" or "Ex Collooney". And when those hard men kicked up a shindy on the train, on their way to and fro, the ticket-checker had a name for them.

'Moving along the train, trying to keep the peace, he would enquire who was making the noise. And then, remembering the tickets he had checked, he would say: "Ah-ha, I know. The wild Collooney boys."'

So, according to Philip, it was the strangers passing through who got the local boys the bad name.

That was a good story. Even if it was told to me by a Collooney boy.

From the summit of Slane one can see, among many other matters, the cattle fattening on the rich heart of Meath. And I think of the cattle-drover herding his, or his master's, hoard from the West to the East to put the golden meat on their bones. He was probably at it in the days of St Patrick. But he had to wait for another Patrick to come along, Padraic Colum, before he could find his place in a poem:

And as I Rode by Granard Moat

To Meath of the pastures,
From wet hills by the sea,
Through Leitrim and Longford,
Go my cattle and me.

I hear in the darkness
Their slipping and breathing –
I name them the by-ways
They're to pass without heeding;

Then the wet, winding roads,
Brown bogs with black water,
And my thoughts on white ships
And the King o' Spain's daughter.

O farmer, strong farmer!
You can spend at the fair,
But your face you must turn
To your crops and your care;

And soldiers, red soldiers!
You've seen many lands,
But you walk two by two,
And by captain's commands!

O the smell of the beasts,
The wet wind in the morn,
And the proud and hard earth
Never broken for corn!

And the crowds at the fair,
The herds loosened and blind,
Loud words and dark faces,
And the wild blood behind!

(O strong men with your best
I would strive breast to breast,
I could quiet your herds,
With my words, with your words!)

I will bring you, my kine,
Where there's grass to the knee,

But you'll think of scant croppings
Harsh with salt of the sea.

Far from the land and the wet roads of the drover, and in one of the most stylish parts of New York City, Padraic Colum and his wife, Mary, had an apartment that would have dazzled a prince. On the Hallowe'en of 1964 I was honoured to enter, with some friends, that exquisite apartment to see Padraic surrounded by admirers and resting at his ease. So I quoted: and, since we were dear friends, no offence was taken at my harmless satire:

OLD WOMAN OF THE ROADS

Oh, to have a little house!
To own the hearth and stool and all!
The heaped-up sods upon the fire,
The pile of turf against the wall!

To have a clock with weights and chains
And pendulum swinging up and down,
A dresser filled with shining delph,
Speckled and white and blue and brown!

I could be busy all the day
Clearing and sweeping hearth and floor,
And fixing on their shelf again
My white and blue and speckled store!

I could be quiet there at night
Beside the fire and myself,
Sure of a bed and loth to leave
The ticking clock and the shining delph!

Och! but I'm weary of mist and dark,
And roads where there's never a house nor bush,
And tired I am of bog and road,
And the crying wind and the lonesome hush!

And I am praying to God on high,
And I am praying him night and day,
For a little house, a house of my own –
out of the wind's and the rain's way.

Padraic Colum used to say, in pleasant jest yet with a certain sort of nostalgia, that he had grown up in Longford Workhouse. The joke was partly about his stature, for he was not a very tall man. His father had been Master of the establishment then sadly so-called. And the little boy growing up under its shadow acquired very early an understanding of and deep sympathy for the ways and trials of the homeless poor.

Perhaps his mind was already absorbed, as a sort of escape, in the wonder-tales that he used so beautifully in that splendid book for the young of all ages, *The King of Ireland's Son*. And he had a regard for Nora Hopper's poem of the same title, which here follows:

Now all away to Tir na n'Og are many roads that run,
But he had ta'en the longest lane, the King of Ireland's son.

There's roads of hate, and roads of love, and many a middle way,
And castles keep the valleys deep where happy lovers stray –

Where Aongus goes there's many a rose burns red 'mid shadows dun,
No rose there is will draw his kiss, the King of Ireland's son.

And yonder, where the sun is high, Love laughs amid the hay,
But smile and sigh have passed him by, and never make delay.

And here (and O! the sun is low) they're glad for harvest won,
But naught he cares for wheat or tares, the King of Ireland's son!

And you have flung love's apple by, and I'm to pluck it yet:
But what are fruits of gramarye with Druid dews beset?

Oh, what are magic fruits to him who meets the Leanan-sidhe
Or hears athwart the distance dim Fionn's horn blow drowsily!

He follows on for ever when all your chase is done,
He follows after shadows, the King of Ireland's son.

And now that that happy little piece has, I hope, put us in the mood, let us listen to the sweep of the scythe in an Irish field, in Michael Cavanagh's translation into the Béarla.

In the original the sweeping scything sound is even more distinct:

A DAY IN IRELAND

Four sharp scythes sweeping – in concert keeping
The rich-robed meadow's broad bosom o'er.
Four strong men mowing with bright health glowing,
A long green sward spread each man before.
With sinews springing – my keen blade swinging –
I strode – the fourth man in that blithe band;
As stalk of corn that summer morn,
The scythe felt light in my stalwart hand.

Oh, King of Glory! How changed my story
Since in youth's noontide – long, long ago,
I mowed that meadow – no cloudy shadow
Between my brow and the hot sun's glow;
Fair girls raking the hay – and making
The fields resound with their laugh and glee,
Their voices ringing – than cuckoo's singing,
Made music sweeter by far to me.

Bees hovered over the honied clover,
Then nestward hied upon wings of light;
No use in trying to trace them flying –
One brief low hum and they're out of sight.
On downy thistle bright insects nestle,
Or flutter skyward on painted wings,
At times alighting on flowers inviting –
'Twas pleasant watching the airy things.

From hazel bushes came songs of thrushes
And blackbirds – sweeter than harper's lay;
While high in ether – with sun-tipped feather –
The skylark warbled his anthem gay;
With throats distended, sweet linnets blended
A thousand notes in one glorious chime,
Oh, King Eternal, 'twas life supernal
In beauteous Erin, that pleasant time.

'I begin through the grass once again to be bound to the Lord,' AE wrote in what can only be considered as the beginning of a prayer. And he might have liked the music of the scythe in 'An Spealadóir' even if he might also have mourned that the grass, the work of the Lord, could ever be sacrilegiously cut down by the hand of man.

But here is AE away in the West in Erris and Tyrawley where the gorse and the heather defy man. Or did until recently. Man becomes more murderous.

CARROWMORE

It's a lonely road through bogland to the lake at Carrowmore,
And a sleeper there lies dreaming where the water laps the shore;
Though the moth-wings of the twilight in their purples are unfurled,
Yet his sleep is filled with music by the Master of the World.

There's a hand is white as silver that is fondling with his hair:
There are glimmering feet of sunshine that are dancing by him there:
And half-open lips of faery that were dyed a faery red
In their revels where the Hazel tree its holy clusters shed.

'Come away,' the red lips whisper, 'all the world is weary now;
'Tis the twilight of the ages and it's time to quit the plough.
Oh, the very sunlight's weary ere it lightens up the dew,
And its gold is changed and faded before it falls to you.

'Though your colleen's heart be tender, a tenderer heart is near.
What's the starlight in her glances when the stars are shining clear?
Who would kiss the fading shadow when the flower-face glows above?
'Tis the beauty of all Beauty that is calling for your love.'

Oh! the great gates of the mountain have opened once again,
And the sound of song and dancing falls upon the ears of men,
And the Land of Youth lies gleaming, flushed with rainbow light and
     mirth,
And the old enchantment lingers in the honey-heart of earth.

And now that we are in the Far West we must find somebody to sing the song that begins on the deck of

Patrick Lynch's boat. In my experience the best man ever to sing it was a Louisburgh man, Austin McDonnell, who was one of the chiefs of the Dublin Fire Brigade. He is no longer with us. But his fine and resounding tenor still stays in my ears, and his generous friendship in my heart. He had a fine patriotic life-story and an enduring affection for his own native places.

This translation from the Irish is generally attributed to a young man called George Fox, a friend of the poet Samuel Ferguson. Fox died far from home, away in South America, and one may feel that Ferguson worked hard to keep alive the name and fame of his young friend.

Here is a note on the poem by Edward Hayes in his valuable nineteenth-century book *The Ballads of Ireland*:

This specimen of our ancient Irish Literature is one of the most popular songs of the peasantry of the counties of Mayo and Galway, and is evidently a composition of the seventeenth century. The original Irish, which is the composition of one Thomas Lavelle, has been published, without a translation, by Mr Hardiman, in his *Irish Minstrelsy*; but a very able translation of it was published by Mr Ferguson, in a review of that work in the 'University Magazine' for June, 1834. The original melody of the same name is of very great beauty and pathos and one which it is desirable to preserve with English words of appropriate simplicity of character.

THE COUNTY OF MAYO

On the deck of Patrick Lynch's boat I sat in woeful plight,
Through my sighing all the weary day, and weeping all the night,
Were it not that full of sorrow from my people forth I go,
By the blessed sun, 'tis royally I'd sing thy praise, Mayo.

When I dwelt at home in plenty, and my gold did much abound,
In the company of fair young maids the Spanish ale went round –
'Tis a bitter change from those gay days that now I'm forced to go,
And must leave my bones in Santa Cruz, far from my own Mayo.

They are altered girls in Irrul now; 'tis proud they're grown and high,
With their hair-bags and their top-knots, for I pass their buckles by –

But it's little now I heed their airs, for God will have it so,
That I must depart for foreign lands, and leave my sweet Mayo.

'Tis my grief that Patrick Loughlin is not Earl in Irrul still,
And that Brian Duff no longer rules as Lord upon the hill;
And that Colonel Hugh Mac Grady should be lying dead and low,
And I sailing, sailing swiftly from the county of Mayo.

Jack Butler Yeats, great painter and most memorable gentleman, liked that old song, and all its Connacht connotations, so much that he called one of his strange, and most diverting, works of prose-fiction simply 'Sailing, Sailing Swiftly'. For Jack Yeats was not only a great painter but a great writer – as Samuel Beckett would always have been the first man to say.

And Jack Yeats had cast his painter's and writer's eye on the Sporting Races of Galway and would always have welcomed the song that celebrated those Races.

It has been said that many's the man went to Galway for the Races and never got as far as Ballybritt, where the horses are, but was delayed by good company in and around Eyre Square. That could be. I was there myself at the races and saw the horses.

Anyhow: listen to the song.

GALWAY RACES

It's there you'll see confectioners with sugar sticks and dainties,
The lozenges and oranges, lemonade and the raisins;
The gingerbread and spices to accommodate the ladies,
And a big crubeen for threepence to be picking while you're able.

It's there you'll see the gamblers, the thimbles and the garters,
And the sporting Wheel of Fortune with the four and twenty quarters,
There was others without scruple pelting wattles at poor Maggy,
And her father well contented and he looking at his daughter.

It's there you'll see the pipers and fiddlers competing,
And the nimble-footed dancers and they tripping on the daisies.

There was others crying segars and lights, and bills of all the races,
With the colour of the jockeys, the prize and horses' ages.

It's there you'll see the jockeys and they mounted on most stately,
The pink and blue, the red and green, the Emblem of our nation.
When the bell was rung for starting, the horses seemed impatient,
Though they never stood on ground, their speed was so amazing.

There was half a million people there of all denominations,
The Catholic, the Protestant, the Jew and Presbyterian.
There was yet no animosity, no matter what persuasion,
But fáilte and hospitality, inducing fresh acquaintance.

Beyond any shadow of a doubt we are now in the West,
where again we encounter the ghost of James Clarence
Mangan. You may meet Mangan, or his ghost, in the
strangest places.

But, here and now, he allows us to share his vision of
Connacht in the thirteenth century, and of Cáhal Mór of
the Wine-Red Hand:

I walked entranced
Through a land of Morn;
The sun, with wondrous excess of light,
Shone down and glanced
Over seas of corn,
And lustrous gardens aleft and right.
Even in the clime
Of resplendent Spain
Beams no such sun upon such a land;
But it was the time,
'Twas in the reign,
Of Cáhal Mór of the Wine-red Hand.

Anon stood nigh
By my side a man
Of princely aspect and port sublime.
Him queried I,
'O, my Lord and Khan,
What clime is this, and what golden time?'

When he – 'The clime
Is a clime to praise,
The clime is Erin's
The green and bland;
And it is the time,
These be the days,
Of Cáhal Mór of the Wine-red Hand.

Then saw I thrones,
And circling fires,
And a Dome rose near me, as by a spell,
Whence flowed the tones
Of silver lyres
And many voices in wreathed swell;
And their thrilling chime
Fell on mine ears
As the heavenly hymn of an angel-band –
'It is now the time,
These be the years,
Of Cáhal Mór of the Wine-red Hand.

I sought the hall,
And, behold! – a change
From light to darkness, from joy to woe!
Kings, nobles, all,
Looked aghast and strange;
The minstrel-group sat in dumbest show!
Had some great crime
Wrought this dread amaze,
This terror? None seemed to understand!
'Twas then the time,
We were in the days,
Of Cáhal Mór of the Wine-red Hand.

I again walked forth;
But lo! the sky
Showed fleckt with blood, and an alien sun
Glared from the north,
And there stood on high,
Amid his shorn beams A SKELETON!
It was by the stream

Of the castled Maine,
One Autumn eve, in the Teuton's land,
That I dreamed this dream
Of the time and reign
Of Cáhal Mór of the Wine-red Hand!

Closer to home and the hearth, though, and far away
from the formidable lands of ancient kings, are the lovely
lines that Douglas Hyde translated and rendered in his *Love
Songs of Connacht*:

Ringleted youth of my love,
With thy locks bound loosely behind thee,
You passed by the road above,
but you never came in to find me;
Where were the harm for you
If you came for a little to see me;
Your kiss is a wakening dew
Were I ever so ill or so dreamy.

If I had a golden store,
I would make a nice little boreen,
To lead straight up to his door,
The door of the house of my storeen;
Hoping to God not to miss
The sound of his footfall in it,
I have waited so long for his kiss
That for days I have slept not a minute.

I thought O my love! you were so —
As the moon is, or sun on a fountain,
And I thought after that you were snow,
The cold snow on the top of the mountain;
And I thought after that you were more
Like God's lamp shining to find me,
Or the bright star of knowledge before,
And the star of wisdom behind me.

You promised me high-heeled shoes,
And satin and silk, my storeen,
And to follow me, never to lose,

Though the ocean were round us roaring;
Like a bush in a gap in a wall
I am now left lonely without thee,
And this house I grow dead of, is all
That I see around or about me.

And since we are in touch with Douglas Hyde, and I
once had the privilege of standing in his presence, it would
be ill-mannered to pass by without recalling those most
moving lines he wrote to the memory of that majestic man,
the great Fenian John O'Mahony. Hyde broods on the
broodings of O'Mahony in exile:

In a foreign land, in a lonesome city,
With few to pity or know or care,
I sleep each night while my heart is burning,
And wake each morning to new despair.

Let no one venture to ask my story
Who believes in glory or trusts to fame;
Yet! I have within me such demons in keeping
As are better sleeping without a name.

For many a day of blood and horror,
And night of terror and work of dread,
I have rescued nought but my honour only,
And this aged, lonely, and whitening head.

Not a single hope have I seen fulfilled
For the blood we spilled when we cast the die;
And the future we painted in brightness and pride
Has the present belied, and shall still belie.

In this far-off country, this city dreary,
I languished weary, and sad, and sore,
Till the flower of youth in glooms o'ershaded
Grew seared, and faded for evermore.

Oh my land! from thee driven – our old flag furled –
I renounced the world when I went from thee;
My heart lingers still on its native strand,
And American land holds nought for me.

Through a long life contriving, hoping, striving,
Driven and driving, leading and led;
I have rescued nought but my honour only,
And this aged, lonely, and whitening head.

There is a West beyond the Irish West. Shane Leslie wrote
well about the work of William Carleton, the contriver of
the *Traits and Stories of the Irish Peasantry*: 'He caught his
types before Ireland made the greatest plunge in her history
and the Famine had cleaned her to the bone. For the
hardiest of the Race rose up and went away into the West,
of which their storytellers had been telling them for a
thousand years.'

Gerald Griffin, a poet and novelist from the same period
as Carleton, but a very, very different sort of man, wrote his
own version of the legend of the dreamer who sailed from
our West to seek the Promised Land or Ultima Thule or the
Isle of the Blest. (Griffin himself gave up the search and
joined the Irish Christian Brothers to find his own Isle of the
Blest.)

On the ocean that hollows the rocks where ye dwell,
A shadowy land has appeared, as they tell;
Men thought it a region of sunshine and rest,
And they called it Hy-Brasil, the isle of the Blest,
From year unto year on the ocean's blue rim,
The beautiful spectre showed lovely and dim;
The golden clouds curtained the deep where it lay,
And it looked like an Eden, away, far away!

A peasant who heard of the wonderful tale,
In the breeze of the Orient loosened his sail;
From Ara, the holy, he turned to the west,
For though Ara was holy, Hy-Brasil was blest.
He heard not the voices that called from the shore –
He heard not the rising wind's menacing roar;
Home, kindred, and safety, he left on that day,
And he sped to Hy-Brasil, away, far away.

Moon rose on the deep, and that shadowy isle,
O'er the faint rim of distance reflected its smile;
Noon burned on the wave, and that shadowy shore
Seemed lovelily distant, and faint as before;
Lone evening came down on the wanderer's track,
And to Ara again he looked timidly back;

Rash dreamer, return! O ye winds of the main,
Bear him back to his own peaceful Ara again.
Rash fool! for a vision of fanciful bliss
To barter thy calm life of labour and peace.
The warning of reason was spoken in vain,
He never re-visited Ara again!
Night fell on the deep, amidst tempest and spray,
And he died on the waters, away, far away.

And now that we have entreated Gerald Griffin to join us
on the Road Round Ireland, let us allow him to celebrate
the lovely Limerick land he came from:

O sweet Adare! O lovely vale!
O soft retreat of sylvan splendour!
Nor summer sun, nor morning gale,
E'er hailed a scene more softly tender.
How shall I tell the thousand charms
Within thy verdant bosom dwelling,
Where, lulled in Nature's fostering arms,
Soft peace abides and joy excelling!

Ye morning airs, how sweet at dawn
The slumbering boughs your song awakens,
Or linger o'er the silent lawn,
With odour of the harebell taken!
Thou rising sun, how richly gleams
Thy smile from far Knockfierna's mountain,
O'er waving woods and bounding streams,
And many a grove and glancing fountain!

Ye clouds of noon, how freshly there,
When summer heats the open meadows,
O'er parched hill and valley fair,
All coolly lie your veiling shadows!

Ye rolling shades and vapours grey,
Slow creeping o'er the golden haven,
How soft ye seal the eye of day,
And wreath the dusky brow of even!

In sweet Adare the jocund Spring
His notes of odorous joy is breathing;
The wild birds in the woodland sing,
The wild flowers in the vale are wreathing.
There winds the Maigue, as silver-clear,
Among the elms so sweetly flowing;
There, fragrant in the early year,
Wild roses on the bank are blowing.

The wild-duck seeks the sedgy bank,
Or dives beneath the glistening billow,
Where graceful droop, and glistening dank,
The osier bright and rustling willow.
The hawthorn scents the leafy dale,
In thicket lone the stag is belling,
And sweet along the echoing vale
The sound of vernal joy is swelling.

Gerald Griffin was a brooding sort of man and much possessed by death. Or, certainly, when he looked on the Vanities of Life he had a very clear vision of the skull beneath the skin. Which, we may guess, was why he finally burned his manuscripts and turned his back on the world and took to the religious life.

And Griffin, in his time, turned his eyes on a problem that has beset us then and that, God help us, we still have.

At that time it was as far to the south as the fine town of Bandon which then had a strong name for what, for some odd reason, is still called Loyalism:

ORANGE AND GREEN

The night was falling dreary,
In merry Bandon town,
When, in his cottage weary,

And as I Rode by Granard Moat

An Orangeman lay down.
The summer sun in splendour
Had set upon the vale,
And shouts of 'No surrender!'
Arose upon the gale.

Beside the waters, laving
The feet of aged trees,
The Orange banners waving,
Flew boldly in the breeze –
In mighty chorus meeting,
A hundred voices join,
And fife and drum were beating
The Battle of the Boyne.

Ha! toward his cottage hieing,
What form is speeding now,
From yonder thicket flying,
With blood upon his brow?
'Hide – hide me, worthy stranger,
Though green my colour be,
And, in the day of danger,
May Heaven remember thee!

'In yonder vale contending,
Alone against that crew,
My life and limbs defending,
An Orangemen I slew;
Hark! hear that fearful warning,
There's death in every tone –
O save my life till morning,
And Heaven prolong your own!'

The Orange heart was melted
In pity to the Green;
He heard the tale, and felt it
His very soul within.
'Dread not that angry warning
Though death be in its tone –
I'll save your life till morning,
Or I will lose my own.'

From Leinster to Connacht

Now, round his lowly dwelling,
The angry torrent pressed,
A hundred voices swelling,
The Orangeman addressed –
'Arise, arise, and follow
The chase along the plain!
In yonder stony hollow
Your only son is slain!'

With rising shouts they gather
Upon the track amain,
And leave the childless father
Aghast with sudden pain.
He seeks the righted stranger
In covert where he lay –
'Arise!' he said, 'all danger
Is gone and past away.

'I had a son – one only,
One loved as my life,
Thy hand has left me lonely,
In that accursed strife.
I pledged my word to save thee
Until the storm should cease,
I keep the pledge I gave thee –
Arise, and go in peace!'

The stranger soon departed
From that unhappy vale;
The father, broken-hearted,
Lay brooding o'er that tale.
Full twenty summers after
To silver turned his beard,
And yet the sound of laughter
From him was never heard.

The night was falling dreary
In merry Wexford town,
When, in his cabin, weary,
A peasant laid him down.
And many a voice was singing
Along the summer vale,

And as I Rode by Granard Moat

And Wexford town was ringing
With shouts of 'Granua Uaile!'

Beside the waters, laving
The feet of aged trees,
The green flag, gaily waving,
Was spread against the breeze –
In mighty chorus meeting,
Loud voices filled the town,
And fife and drum were beating,
'Down, Orangemen, lie down!'

Hark, 'mid the stirring clangour
That woke the echoes there,
Loud voices, high in anger,
Rise on the evening air.
Like billows of the ocean,
He sees them hurry on –
And, 'mid the wild commotion,
An Orangeman alone.

'My hair,' he said, 'is hoary,
And feeble is my hand,
And I could tell a story
Would shame your cruel band.
Full twenty years and over
Have changed my heart and brow,
And I am grown a lover
Of peace and concord now.

'It was not thus I greeted your
Brother of the green;
When fainting and defeated
I freely took him in.
I pledged my word to save him,
From vengeance rushing on,
I kept the pledge I gave him,
Though he had killed my son.'

That aged peasant heard him,
And knew him as he stood;
Remembrance kindly stirred him,

And tender gratitude.
With gushing tears of pleasure,
He pierced the listening train,
'I'm here to pay the measure
Of kindness back again!'

Upon his bosom falling,
That old man's tears came down;
Deep memory recalling
That cot and fatal town.
'The hand that would offend thee,
My being first shall end;
I'm living to defend thee,
My saviour and my friend!'

He said, and slowly turning,
Addressed the wondering crowd;
With fervent spirit burning,
He told the tale aloud.
Now pressed the warm beholders,
Their aged foe to greet;
They raised him on their shoulders
And chaired him through the street.

As he had saved that stranger
From peril scowling dim,
So in his day of danger
Did Heaven remember him.
By joyous crowds attended,
The worthy pair were seen,
And their flags that day were blended
Of Orange and of Green.

And may we yet live to see the day.

But the mystery land, the West beyond our West, still
beckons ...

Griffin's hapless Aranmore may have died on the waters,
away far away, but inevitably, a cute Kerryman by the name
of Brendan did, according to all accounts, discover the
enchanted land, beating to its magic shores not only

Columbus but even the hardy Norse sea-rovers. Francis
MacManus, the novelist, celebrated that saintly rover, and
the Munster mountain named after him, in one of his few
poems:

PATTERN OF SAINT BRENDAN

This is an evening for a hallowed landfall,
The landbreeze slithers down Brandon
Mountain where stone on stone the monkhives
crumble and no prayers drone since twelve evangels
voyaged to find the summer islands.
The light withdraws over the maudlin village
and upended curraghs upended like black cattle,
to follow the copper Atlantic shimmer.
O how could twelve exiles
return from voyaging, staring at wonders and charting
infinity, and raise dripping oars to glide
rejoicing, chanting laudate with salty lips cracking,
back from the peril of where the sun founders,
to search for lost Ireland round their cold mountain.

This is the evening. The bleat of melodeons
buckleaps fandangos and whips
up the hobnails to belt at the floorboards.
Thirst gravels the gullet; lads with puffed faces
muster a yowl for slopped foamy porter
and grope for the pence in the fist-hoarded purses.
Fug blears the wicks; the sergeant is strutting,
tunic neck-open, bellyband bursting;
Annastatia and Nellie slip off to go pairing
at a tip and a wink to the back of the graveyard.
Goat-music, fumes, the stamp of wild heel-bones,
dust whirling high with the din and the fag-smoke,
cries for a fight and calls for the sergeant,
the anger of louts for a gombeenman's farthing,
follow the dayfall, out to the foundered
islands desired from bleak Brandon Mountain.

This is the evening, Brendan, O sailor,
stand off the mainland, backwater the glimmer,
though kirtles be flittered and flesh be seasalted;
watch while this Ireland, a mirage, grows dimmer.
What have you come for? Why cease from faring
through paradise islands and indigo water,
through vinland and bloomland and Caribbean glory?
Follow your chart with the smoky sea-monsters;
stay with the bright birds where music is pouring
balm for the hurt souls, and Judas repentant
sits for one day on a rock in the ocean.
Turn from the ghostland, O great navigator;
lower the oars for a legend
of journeys; scan tossed
empty horizons from pole to equator
for Ireland, time-foundered, that Ireland has lost.

Well, once you got to the far side of the great ocean it was imperative that you find your way back again to time-foundered Ireland. Three times, I am happy to say, I did it on grand ocean-liners and never shall I forget the excitement of seeing the great headlands of the south-west reaching out over the waves as if to embrace you and welcome you home.

For obvious reasons that return cannot be the same by jet airliner. But you may remember that movie about the heroic Charles Lindbergh, *The Spirit of St Louis*. When the solo flyer came in over our south-west he could see Ireland, as the movie showed us, and very glad he was to see it. Planes, at that time, flew lower and slower.

But when, from the decks of those three ocean-liners, I saw the Irish headlands, I quoted to myself, or to anyone who would listen to me, Thomas D'Arcy McGee's sad, yet triumphant, lines about the aged man, homeward bound, on a slower ship and a long time ago.

And as I Rode by Granard Moat

THE HOMEWARD BOUND

Paler and thinner the morning moon grew,
Colder and sterner the rising wind blew;
The pole-star had set in a forest of cloud,
And the icicles crackled on spar and on shroud,
When a voice from below we heard feebly cry:
'Let me see, let me see my own land ere I die.

'Ah, dear sailor, say, have we sighted Cape Clear?
Can you see any sign? Is the morning light near?
You are young, my brave boy; thanks, thanks for your hand –
Help me up, till I get a last glimpse of the land.
Thank God, 'tis the sun that now reddens the sky;
I shall see, I shall see my own land ere I die.

'Let me lean on your strength, I am feeble and old,
And one half of my heart is already stone-cold.
Forty years work a change! when I first crossed the sea
There were few on the deck that could grapple with me;
But my youth and my prime in Ohio went by,
And I'm come back to see the old spot ere I die.'

'Twas a feeble old man, and he stood on the deck,
His arm round a kindly young mariner's neck,
His ghastly gaze fixed on the tints of the east,
As a starveling might stare at the sight of a feast.
The morn quickly rose and revealed to his eye
The land he had prayed to behold, and then die!

Green, green was the shore, though the year was near done;
High and haughty the capes the white surf dashed upon;
A grey ruined convent was down by the strand,
And the sheep fed afar, on the hills of the land!
'God be with you, dear Ireland!' he gasped with a sigh;
'I have lived to behold you – I'm ready to die.'

He sank by the hour, and his pulse 'gan to fail,
As we swept by the headland of storied Kinsale;
Off Ardigna Bay it came slower and slower,
And his corpse was clay-cold as we sighted Tramore.
At Passage we waked him, and now he doth lie
In the lap of the land he beheld but to die.

162

The desire for home that moves and torments the exile is an historic and unavoidable part of our inheritance. Winifred Letts, a gentle lady-poet from the south-east, did tenderly reflect on it:

> I think if I lay dying in some land
> Where Ireland is no more than just a name,
> My soul would travel back to find that strand
> From whence it came.
>
> I'd see the harbour in the evening light,
> The old man staring at some distant ship,
> The fishing-boats they fasten left and right
> Beside the slip.
>
> The sea-wrack lying on the wind-swept shore,
> The grey thorn bushes growing in the sand,
> Our Wexford coast from Arklow to Cahore –
> My native land.
>
> The little houses climbing up the hill.
> Sea daisies growing in the sandy grass,
> The tethered goats that wait large-eyed and still
> To watch you pass.
>
> The women at the well with dripping pails,
> Their men colloguing by the harbour walls,
> The coils of rope, the nets, the old brown sails
> I know them all.
>
> And then the Angelus – I'd surely see
> The swaying bell against a golden sky,
> So God, Who kept the love of home in me,
> Would let me die.

And now to find, perhaps, the Ireland the exiles wished to return to. Francis MacManus, as I have said, occasionally allowed himself to relax into verse. And here he is praising his own country in words that he entitled 'Excerpts from an Irish Sequence':

Praise God for Ireland, so – he said,
and raised his hand;
a poet he was whose withered heart and head
had one time answered as one cry
to every stir and sigh
of the quick, and the importunate dead,
to the windy fields and the high
desolate places of the isolate, seathundering, wrysmiling land;
he raised his hand:
Praise God, – says he,
calling a ritual, twofingered blessing
as from a liturgy.

Therefore, like daybreak, let his wishing spread
from here to the tufted sands,
and the shell-bestrewn silver and yellow strands,
from here to the dread
rockresisted charge of the western sea
where lies uncharted mystery;
– spread like the allmothering air
over all your people and mine; over the young and the old,
the dark, swarthy, grey, red and fair,
let the blessing unfold:
on craft and calling, profession and art and trade,
on all who make and all that ever is made;
on thinker, teacher, poet, priest, soldier and clerk,
on farmer, ploughman and herdsman, all who work;
on city and street, as tired as an old shuttered room,
on every long valley whence rivers run down to a tide,
to the quays and the bales and the stealthy slow glide
of the trafficking ships, and the dim muffled boom
of the lusty, the free,
the allfathering sea:
on the fishers who ride
with the nets in the night
above forests of weed and the round
immaculate shining white
bones of the drowned
bedded deep,
unrotten,

From Leinster to Connacht

forgotten
in sleep.

Praise God for Ireland, so – says he,
and raised a blessing as from a liturgy.

Asleep is the street. One solitary cart rattles out.
The hot sweaty face of the driver is dark in the dusk.
He thumps the creel with his fist and out of his mouth rolls the brusque
bedamning abuse of the drinker who named him a lout;
and he settles his cap with a rakish jerk of his thumb
and fingers the fob of his vest for the wrack of his pounds,
and sways and grows wroth and mutters how beggarly hounds
would drink your health deep as long as the money would come.
The mare has her head; and drowsy and bothered he hears
the fair's hollow hubbub
since cockcrow at cold showery morn
with one thrush on the thorn
to the arguments, squabbles and jeers
in the dark crowded pub.
Good morrow! God save you! I wouldn't be seen with the beast!
The lowing of cattle creeps mistily up through the air.
I'll not drink another. Enough is as good as a feast.
By God, there's not much as a hap'orth to do on this fair.
Come all ye lads and lassies, and listen to me awhile.
This drink has me ruined, but come, man, a half-one or ale?
If Dublin would leave us alone we'd ride grandly in style.
Push up on the bench and listen to this for a tale.

Praise.
The stars weave a tale. A parish is belled up from sleep
by the howl of a dog that leaps to the walk of the dead;
the howl calls replies; and mongrels by tinkers' fires creep
from the tents and the vans, and prowl on the stiff legs of dread.
And deep in a ditchful of ferns, cracked itchy Tom Straw
plucks his rags with the cold and clutches his dirty black cans;
'O Jesus, protect me,' prays he, 'they'll not credit I saw
the grand lady's ghost and held her poor hands in my hands.'

Praise.
A train rumbling east trails a palely lit smoke through a glen.
There's flame in the sky where the Liffey retreats from the tide.

And as I Rode by Granard Moat

The day fills the fields where the shiny damp cattle complain.
Slow over Allen the clouds with the rainlances ride.
How many men for Dublin?
Six men and ten,
shot in the dawnlight,
called to life again.
Wake up the mansions,
wake up the slums,
wake up the navvies,
mickeydazzlers, jems,
paperboys and joxers,
polismen and tarts,
butchers and bakers,
bankers and clerks,
dockers and coalmen,
milkmen and maids,
civilservants, busmen,
drapers and drays.
Steam up the hooters,
light is in the east, open up the churchdoors,
here comes the priest.
How many men for Dublin?
There they walk again!
Rebels in the ruinlight,
six men and ten.

Praise.
Ireland's a rock that men scoop out for their bread;
Ireland's a door where the living collogue with the dead;
Ireland's a river, a valley, a young nation, an old,
a house guarded by heroes, a fair where heroes are sold.
Ireland's a sow that farrows; then feeds on her young;
Ireland's a queen for all the fine songs that were sung;
Ireland's a speech, a mouthful of words cried in rage
by a rebel who gets a hempen cravat as his wage.
Ireland's a south wind, a west wind, a blowing wet morn,
a ridge of potatoes, ditches, a few roods of corn.
Ireland's a priest with a chalice, a scourge and a bell;
a monk who prays prone on the stony floor of his cell;
a singer's regret, a dream of an exile who makes

a hovel a castle, and princes of randy old rakes.
Ireland's a pasture where men are measured by breed,
Ireland's a ploughman, a plough, and a handful of seed.

Praise God, – says he,
spreading a ritual twofingered blessing
as from a liturgy.

Let us stay for a bit with Francis MacManus. He was always
good company. And now that he has brought us back to
Ireland, and Mayo, we can, in his company, watch the
pilgrims climbing the Reek. Twice in my life I was among
those pilgrims. That was away back when I was able to walk.

Then from the Reek, and St Patrick, MacManus will
bring us to the Oak of Kildare and St Brigid.

And then to the tragic, and splendid, city of Limerick.
There's a lot of history around Limerick, as any Limerick-
man, or any man from anywhere, can tell you. But first to
the Reek:

ASCENT OF THE REEK

Pilgrims, O pilgrims, where are you going?
Up to the Reek, to the holy man's mountain.
Keep your stick in your fist or you'll tumble forever,
tumble and toss with the torrents of water,
water that's brown with the bog's bitter drainings,
water that scours out the rocks like a penance.
But Patrick keeps guard from the cold windy summit,
watching with prayer like the sunrise about him,
his casula wet with the labour of sorrow,
his bell hoarse with ringing damnation to demons,
for fear we should fail, we the nation he fashioned;
watching forever, his eyes never weary,
wrestling with devils and angels and Heaven,
he, who accounted himself sinner of sinners.

Pilgrims, O pilgrims, how far to the summit?
Now our breath breaks like the shudder of death,

now the sharp stones are an ambush of demons,
now the cold morning cuts heat from our hearts.

Pilgrims, O pilgrims, the darkness is lifting,
daybreak is polishing ocean's dulled mirror,
islands will gleam like the rivets on silver.
But prayers must be said till the heart groans in anguish,
limbs must be strained till the flesh is no rebel,
bones must be tried till the will is the master,
slopes must be climbed till the body is civil.
Thirst is a prayer that makes the tongue kindle;
hunger a penance that cries in the belly.
Pilgrims, O pilgrims, look down on the ocean,
morning uncovers the islands to glory.

Pilgrims, O pilgrims, here is your haven.
Lost are the torrents spuming sour water;
below is the bog that hugged the heels evilly;
below are the boulders that huddled to hinder us;
below are the flints that dared us and prattled.
But look to that man who bares his knees bravely,
kneels to the stones while his mouth mutters Aves.
(God save ye, pilgrims, here Patrick guards us!)

Look at that woman, old as the mountain,
swinging her beads to the shake of her fingers.
(Patrick is watching over all Ireland)
Look at that girl who skips like a sparrow,
brown as a berry, laughing and gabbing.
Patrick he guards them all from his mountain,
guarding with prayers like those strong winds about him,
his casula wet with the love that melts heaven,
his bell beating devils to rout in infernos,
for fear we should fail, we his nation, his people,
watching for ever, his eyes like the planets,
Patrick the slave and the master of Ireland.

Pilgrims, O pilgrims, whence are you coming?
Back from Croagh Patrick's mountain high vigil.
Back from the flight of the darkness at morning.
Back from a word to the maker of Ireland.

From Leinster to Connacht

All night the woods were talking:
colloquy of nodding heads till matins
levelled light through sparkling bracken,
caught the tardy poachers napping,
teased the convent cocks to bragging,
and hushed blown boughs with the din of morning.

All night the trees colloguing,
mouth to ear, implored an answer.
'Tell, O tell, who was she walking, daring
dayfall to a candle,'
murmured gravely swaying elms;
'probing thistledown alighting were less
gentle than her sandals.'

Beeches swung like happy bellmen:
'Over in the claustral brambles
blackbirds tucked up drooping habits,
chirped and hurried, drowsy
brethren badgered by a prowling
abbot; hurried, ranked the boughs, sang,
and sang, weaving light above the pathway
till the woods with glim-note, hymn-flame, star-chant,
song-flare ran and rang.'
'She,' the ash said.
– a skitting whisper –
'is a king's maid,
a chieftain's surely,
slipped through a dun-gate
to inveigle a lover.'
'Look!' cried the yew, 'but those skulking trappers
will creep empty-satchelled back to their slatterns,
and search for the hag whose viper cursing
poisoned the night for snaring and netting.
Who can forget the warren folk's merriment,
eyes like the sun on dew-polished berries,
ripe to the glint of no curse but her blessing?'

'Who?' sighed the woods.

'Who?' all together,

Thus all night the woods were talking,
a colloquy of nodding heads since vespers.
Only the oak knew Brighid the bright nun walking,
mothering as evening air,
through the flocked glebe-land and among the talking
trees in windy, cropped Kildare.

ST JOHN'S TOWER, LIMERICK

Only the Shannon's hurtling water,
only these ramparts that crannied lichens climb,
can tell how fighters fled from sterile slaughter,
and God intoned Amen to their time.
River, tell me, river, did a nation topple when swordsmen
wrestled with the ladders and tumbled to the pikemen?
Ramparts, tell me, ramparts, was an epoch dust and rubble
when the lords sailed from Ireland to mix in foreign trouble?

Our fathers, are they fathers? Or shadows from a story
finished on these ramparts watching Limerick town,
while we, with empty pockets, pick their purse of glory?
River, tell me, rampart, are we heirs to old renown?
Limerick fell. And this, only this I know,
only a hovelled rabble was left to build from slaughter,
only ruined ramparts where patient grasses grow,
only the Shannon's hurtling water.

I had a friend once, a Jesuit of all things, who highly disapproved of G.K. Chesterton. For this reason: that particular Jesuit did not like long walks. He preferred sitting down, and he said that Chesterton sang the praises of long walks that, fat as Chesterton was, he was never able to take. He was talking and, of course, joking about the ballad about the rolling English road: 'The night we went to Bannockburn by way of Brighton Pier ...' And more of the same.

Perhaps our roundabout road to Granard Moat might, by now, have made some of us footsore. But bear up. And take courage from the lines of C.J. Boland, a sound man from the Suir Valley. And from the conversation he overheard from two travellers.

If you wish, you may sing this to the tune to which Percy French put his meditations on Hannigan's Aunt:

'All over the world,' the traveller said,
'In my wanderings I have been;
But these two lookin' eyes have seen.
From the haunts of the ape an' marmozet,
To the lands of the Fellaheen.'
Says the other, 'I'll lay you an even bet
You were never in Farranaleen.'

'I've hunted the woods of Seringapatam,
An' sailed in the Polar Seas.
I fished for a week in the Gulf of Siam
An' lunched on the Chersonese.
I've lived in the valleys of fair Cashmere,
Under Himalay's snowy ridge.'
Says the other impatiently, 'Looka here,
Were you ever at Laffan's Bridge?'

'I've lived in the land where tobacco is grown,
In the suburbs of Santiago;
An' I spent two years in Sierra Leone,
An' in Terra Del Fuego.
I walked across Panama all in a day,
Ah me, but the road was rocky!'
The other replied, 'Will you kindly say,
Were you ever at Horse-and-Jockey?

'I've borne my part in a savage fray,
When I got this wound from a Lascar;
We were bound just then from Mandalay
For the isle of Madagascar.
Ah! the sun never tired of shining there,
An' the trees canaries sang in.'
'What of that?' says the other, 'Sure I've a pair,
And there's lots more over in Drangan.'

And as I Rode by Granard Moat

'I've hunted tigers in Turkestan,
In Australia the kangaroos;
An' I lived six months as medicine man
To a tribe of Katmandoos.
An' I've stood on the scene of Olympic games,
Where the Grecians showed their paces.'
The other replied, 'Now tell me, James,
Were you ever at Fethard Races?

'Don't talk of your hunting in Yucatan,
Or your fishing off Saint Helena;
I'd rather see young lads hunting the wran
In the hedges of Tubberheena.
No doubt the scenes of a Swiss canton
Have a passable sort of charm,
But give me a sunset on Sliabh na mBan
From the road by Hackett's Farm.

'An' I'd rather be strolling along the quay,
An' watching the river flow,
Than growing tea with the cute Chinee,
Or mining in Mexico.
An' I wouldn't much care for Sierra Leone,
If I hadn't seen Killenaule,
An' the man that ne'er saw Mullinahone
Shouldn't say he had travelled at all.'

IV

From Connacht to Munster

So Boland and his two travellers have, in the best Chestertonian fashion, brought us round the world and back again,
to land us in the heart of Munster, where we may stay for a
while – even in the stimulating if somewhat hazardous company of Robert Dwyer Joyce's Blacksmith of Limerick.

About that blacksmith I have always worried a bit, as I
did about Bold Paudh O'Donoghue when the Yeos were in
Dunshaughlin and the Hessians in Dunrea. Often as I have
been in Dunshaughlin, and frequently in the august
company of Brinsley MacNamara, I never saw one Yeo. But
bold Paudh and his patriotic fellow in Limerick were over-
agile with the hammer. And to this day when I am close to
them I walk with my head averted.

Here now is the Limerck hero:

THE BLACKSMITH OF LIMERICK

He grasped his ponderous hammer, he could not stand it more,
To hear the bombshells bursting, and the thundering battle's roar;
He said – 'The breech they're mounting, the Dutchman's murdering crew –
I'll try my hammer on their heads and see what that can do!

'Now, swarthy Ned and Moran, make up that iron well;
'Tis Sarsfield's horse that wants the shoes, so mind not shot nor shell';
'Ah sure,' cried both, 'the horse can wait – for Sarsfield's on the wall,
And where you go we'll follow, with you to stand or fall!'

The blacksmith raised his hammer, and rushed into the street,
His 'prentice boys behind him, the ruthless foe to meet –

And as I Rode by Granard Moat

High on the breach of Limerick, with dauntless hearts they stood,
Where the bombshells burst, and shot fell thick, and redly ran the blood.

'Now, look you, brown-haired Moran, and mark you, swarthy Ned,
This day we'll prove the thickness of many a Dutchman's head!
Hurrah! upon their bloody path they're mounting gallantly;
And now, the first that tops the breach, leave him to this and me!'

The first that gained the rampart, he was a captain brave!
A captain of the grenadiers, with blood-stained dirk and glaive;
He pointed and he parried, but it was all in vain,
For fast through skull and helmet the hammer found his brain!

The next that topped the rampart, he was a colonel bold,
Bright through the murk of battle his helmet flashed with gold –
'Gold is no match for iron,' the doughty blacksmith said,
As with that ponderous hammer he cracked his foeman's head!

'Hurrah for gallant Limerick!' black Ned and Moran cried,
As on the Dutchman's leaden heads their hammers well they plied;
A bombshell burst between them – one fell without a groan,
One leaped into the lurid air, and down the breach was thrown!

'Brave smith! brave smith!' cried Sarsfield, 'beware the treacherous mine –
Brave smith! brave smith! fall backward, or surely death is thine!'
The smith sprang up the rampart and leaped the blood-stained wall,
As high into the shuddering air went foemen, breach, and all!

Up like a red volcano they thundered wild and high,
Spear, gun, and shattered standard, and foemen through the sky;
And dark and bloody was the shower that round the blacksmith fell –
He thought upon his 'prentice boys, they were avenged well!

On foemen and defenders a silence gathered down,
'Twas broken by a triumph-shout that shook the ancient town;
As out its heroes sallied, and bravely charged and slew,
And taught King William and his men what Irish hearts can do!

Down rushed the swarthy blacksmith unto the river side,
He hammered on the foe's pontoon, to sink it in the tide;
The timber it was tough and strong, it took no crack or strain –
'Mavrone, 'twon't break,' the blacksmith roared, 'I'll try their heads
    again!'

The blacksmith sought his smithy, and blew his bellows strong,
He shod the steed of Sarsfield, but o'er it sang no song:
'Ochón! my boys are dead,' he cried; 'their loss I'll long deplore,
But comfort's in my heart, their graves are red with foreign gore!'

[Robert Dwyer Joyce]

Ouch! And God preserve us. And the moral is: Keep your head down, and keep it in a helmet when you're passing through Limerick.

But now that Patrick Sarsfield has been mentioned, I may have somewhat more to say about him. Or let Denis A. McCarthy say it in his poem about the famous ride to Ballyneety. I have an odd and comical memory about that poem.

A few miles outside my home town there lived William Norris, a small but industrious and prosperous farmer, and his two rosy-cheeked sisters. Willy was a good Orangeman. There was a long-standing friendship that had nothing to do with politics, just friendship and neighbourliness between my parents and the Norris family. So that, off and on, I would be marched out by two of my sisters to visit the lovely Norrises.

And one July, coming up to the Twelfth, I was asked to stand up and recite. And did, being one of those awful little schoolboys who can remember and recite everything, mathematics excepted. I recited every line of what now follows, and Willy's sash hanging up there to air for the great Walk and the great Day.

Unaware I was of the political significance of my performance. Nor had I any wish to offend. And Willy Norris was highly delighted, and afterwards persuaded my elder brother to get him the complete words written down. Which my brother, naturally, did.

Did Willy read them out in the Lodge?

Oh, God be with those happy days!

175

And as I Rode by Granard Moat

Anyway: here are the words:

The night we rode with Sarsfield out from Limerick to meet
The wagon-train that William hoped would help in our defeat,
How clearly I remember it, though now my hair is white
That clustered black and curly 'neath my trooper's cap that night.
For I was one of Sarsfield's men, in years though still a lad,
And to be one of Sarsfield's men what boy would not be glad?
For Sarsfield chose, of all his troops, the best and bravest ones
To ride and raid the convoy's camp that brought the English guns.

'Twas silently we left the town and silently we rode,
While o'er our heads the silent stars in silver beauty glowed.
And silently and stealthily, well led by one who knew,
We crossed the shining Shannon at the ford of Killaloe.
The galloping O'Hogan, Ireland's fiery-hearted son,
'Twas he, by many a byway, led us confidently on,
Till when the night was nearly spent we saw the distant glow
The English convoy's campfire in the quiet vale below.

Still silently and stealthily, at Sarsfield's stern command
We close and closer drew the lines of our devoted band.
'We must not fail, my comrades.' That was Sarsfield's voice that spoke.
'For Limerick and Ireland's fate depend upon this stroke.
The password of the Williamites is Sarsfield. Strange but true.
And with that word upon our lips, we'll pass the sentries through.
Then when you hear my voice upraised, charge boldly, one and all.
No cannon from this convoy e'er must bark at Limerick's wall.'

The sleepy sentry, on his rounds, perhaps was musing o'er
His happy days of childhood on the pleasant English shore.
Perhaps was thinking of his home and wishing he were there,
When springtime makes the English land so wonderfully fair.
At last our horses' hoof-beats and our jingling arms he heard.
'Halt! Who goes there?' the sentry cried: 'Advance and give the word.'
'The word is Sarsfield,' cried our Chief. 'And stop us he who can.
For Sarsfield is the word tonight. And Sarsfield is the man.'

One bursting cheer, one headlong charge, and sabres bright and keen
Are hacking at the foemen's heads where'er a head is seen.
The colonel leaves his wig behind, bestrides a horse and flies
To tell of Sarsfield's daring and the convoy camp's surprise.

From Connacht to Munster

We make a pile of captured guns and powder-bags and stores,
Then skyward in one flaming blast the great explosion roars.
And then we sang, as back we rode with Sarsfield in the van:
'Ho! Sarsfield is the word tonight and Sarsfield is the man.'

The night we rode with Sarsfield, I shall always hold it dear,
Though he is dead on Landen Plain, this many and many a year.
Though he is dead and I am old, my hair all silver white
That clustered black and curly 'neath my trooper's cap that night.
For I was one of Sarsfield's men, while yet a boy in years
I rode as one of Sarsfield's men and men were my compeers.
They're dead, the most of them, afar, yet they were Ireland's sons
Who saved the walls of Limerick from the might of English guns.

But here and now is another Limerick hero. He was first
introduced to me a long long time ago in the columns of
Ireland's Own. His story, as told here, may take up overmuch
space in this assembly: and, perhaps, he should not even be
admitted. But I have a sort of old affection for him and I
can't keep him out. He keeps beating on the door. He may
break it in. He is, I'd say, a blood relation of Tam O'Shan-
ter.

So, come in Drunken Thady and the Bishop's Lady:

DRUNKEN THADY
(a legend of Limerick)

Before the famed year Ninety-eight,
In blood stamp'd Ireland's wayward fate;
When laws of death and transportation
Were served, like banquets, thro' the nation –
But let it pass – the tale I dwell on
Has nought to do with red Rebellion;
Altho' it was a glorious ruction,
And nearly wrought our foes' destruction.
There lived and died in Limerick City,
A dame of fame – Oh! what a pity
That dames of fame should live and die,
And never learn for what, or why!

177

And as I Rode by Granard Moat

Some say her maiden name was Brady,
And others say she was a Grady;
The d___ I choke their contradictions!
For truth is murder'd by their fictions.
'Tis true she lived – 'tis true she died,
'Tis true she was a Bishop's bride,
But for herself, 'tis little matter
To whom she had been wife or daughter.
Whether of Bradys or O'Gradys!
She lived, like most ungodly ladies,
Spending his Reverend Lordship's treasure;
Chasing the world's evil pleasure;
In love with suppers, cards, and balls,
And luxurious sin of festive halls,
Where flaming hearts, and flaming wine,
Invite the passions all to dine.
She died – her actions were recorded –
Whether in Heaven or Hell rewarded
We know not, but her time was given
Without a thought of Hell or Heaven.
Her days and nights were spent in mirth –
She made her genial Heaven of earth;
And never dreamt, at balls and dinners,
There is a Hell to punish sinners.
How quick Time throws his rapid measure
Along the date of wordly pleasure?
A beam of light, 'mid cloudy shadows,
Flitting along the autumn meadows;
A wave that glistens on the shore,
Retires, and is beheld no more;
A blast that stirs the yellow leaves
Of fading woods, in autumn eves;
A star's reflection on the tide,
Which gathering shadows soon shall hide. –
Such and so transient, the condition
Of earthly joys and man's ambition.
Death steals behind the smile of joy,
With weapon ready to destroy;
And, tho' a hundred years were past,
He's sure to have his prey at last.

And, when the fated hour is ready,
He cares not for a lord or lady;
But lifts his gun, and snaps the trigger
And shoots alike the king and beggar.
And thus the heroine of our tale,
He shot, as fowlers shoot a quail;
And, 'mid the flash of pomp and splendour,
He made her soul the world surrender.
She join'd her father's awful forms
'Mid rolling clouds and swelling storms;
And, lest the Muse would be a liar,
I'm led to think she went no higher.
But now I have some secret notion,
She did not like her new promotion;
For if she did she would remain,
And scorn to come to earth again.
But earth, the home of her affection,
Could not depart her recollection!
So she return'd to flash and shine,
But never more to dance or dine!
The story of her resurrection
Flew out in many a queer direction!
Each night, she roam'd, with airy feet,
From Thomond Bridge to Castle-street;
And those that stay'd out past eleven,
Would want a special guard from Heaven,
To shield them, with a holy wand,
From the mad terrors of her hand!
She knock'd two drunken soldiers dead,
Two more, with batter'd foreheads, fled;
She broke the sentry-box in staves,
And dash'd the fragments in the waves!
She slash'd the gunners, left and right,
And put the garrison to flight!
The devil, with all his faults and failings,
Was far more quiet in his dealings
(Notwithstanding all that he lost)
Than this unruly, rampant she-ghost!
No pugilist in Limerick Town,
Could knock a man so quickly down,

Or deal an active blow so ready
To floor one, as the Bishop's Lady!
And thus the ghost appear'd and vanished,
Until her Ladyship was banish'd
By Father Power whom things of evil
Dread as mortals dread the devil!
Off to the Red Sea shore he drove her,
From which no tide nor time can move her,
From numbering sands upon the coast
That skirts the grave of Pharaoh's host!
A lady of her high-born station
Must have acquired great education
For such a clerkship – numbering sands,
With no account-book, save her hands!

But, ere the Priest removed the Lady,
There lived a 'Boy', call'd 'Drunken Thady'!
In Thomond-gate, of social joys,
The birth-place of the 'Devil's Boys'!
Thade knew his country's history well,
And for her sake would go to hell!
For hours he'd sit and madly reason
Upon the honours of high treason!
What Bills the House had lately got in,
What Croppies nimbly danced on nothing!
And how the wily game of State
Was dealt and play'd in Ninety-eight!
How Wexford fought – how Ross was lost!
And all to Erin's bloody cost!
But had the powers of Munster 'risen,
Erin had England by the weasan'!
He told long tales about those play-boys,
Call'd Terry Alts and Peep-o'-day Boys
Who roused, at night, the sleeping country,
And terrified the trembling gentry!

Now who dare say that Irish history
To Thady's breeding was a mystery?
Altho' the Parish Priest proclaim'd him,
And first of living devils named him!
In heart he was an Irish Lumper,

But all his glory was a bumper!
He believed in God, right firm and well,
But served no Heaven and feared no Hell!
A sermon on Hell's pains may start him,
It may convince but not convert him!
He knew his failing and his fault
Lay in the tempting drop of malt;
And every day his vice went further,
And, as he drank, his heart grew harder.
Ah, Thady! oft the Parish Priest
Call'd you a wicked, drunken beast!
And said you were the devil's handle
Of brazen, bare-faced, public scandal!
An imp – without the least contrition –
At whiskey, discord and sedition!
That drinking was your sole enjoyment,
And breaking doors your whole employment!
That you – at every drunken caper –
Made windows change their glass for paper!
That sure as closed each Sunday night in,
You set near half the parish fighting!
That, with your constant, droughty quaffing,
You broke Moll Dea and Biddy Lavin!
And drove the two poor widows begging,
For not a drop you left their keg in!
If Satan stood, with his artillery,
Full at the gates of Stein's Distillery;
With Satan's self you'd stand a tussle
To enter there and wet your whistle!

In vain the Priest reproved his doings –
Even as the ivy holds the ruins –
He caution'd, counsell'd, watch'd and track'd him,
But all in vain – at last he whack'd him;
And with a blackthorn, highly seasoned,
He urged the argument he'd reason'd.
But Thady loved intoxication,
And foil'd all hopes of reformation;
He still rais'd rows and drank the whiskey,
And roar'd, just like the Bay of Biscay.

And as I Rode by Granard Moat

In every grog-shop he was found,
In every row he fought a round;
The treadmill knew his step as well
As e'er a bellman knew his bell;
The jail received him forty times
For midnight rows and drunken crimes;
He flailed his wife and thump'd her brother,
And burn'd the bed about his mother,
Because they hid his fine steel pike
Deep down in Paudh Molony's dike!
The guard was call'd out to arrest him,
Across the quarry loch they chased him;
The night was dark, the path was narrow,
Scarce giving room to one wheelbarrow;
Thade knew the scanty passage well,
But headlong his pursuers fell
Into the stagnant, miry brook
Like birds in birdlime sudden stuck.
The neighbours said the devil steel'd him,
For if the garrison assail'd him
Inside King John's strong Castle-wall,
He would escape unhurt from all!
All day he drank 'potheen' at Hayes's,
And pitched the King and Law to blazes!
He knocked his master on the floor,
And kiss'd Miss Lizzy at the door!
But ere his drunken pranks went further,
The host and he had milla murdher!
The window panes he broke entire
The bottles flew about the fire;
The liquor, on the hearth increasing,
Caught fire and set the chimney blazing!
The Reverend sage this deed admonish'd,
The congregation stood astonish'd –
He said that Thady was an agent
Employ'd on earth by hell's black Regent!
And if he wouldn't soon reform,
His place and pay would be more warm!
His vital thread would soon be nick'd,
And into Hades he'd be kick'd!

Even there he would not be admitted,
Except the Porter he outwitted!
For, if he got inside the wall,
Most likely, he'd out-devil them all!
The people heard the sad assertion,
And pray'd aloud for his conversion!
While Thady in the public-house
Was emptying kegs and 'brewing' rows!
For him the Priest prognosticated
A woeful doom and end ill-fated!
And truth had rarely disappointed
The sayings of the Lord's Anointed!
But many a one in heaven takes dinner,
Who died a saint and lived a sinner!
'Twere better far, and safer surely,
To live a saint and die one purely!
All ye who're ready to condemn
A fellow-child of clay, like him!
Try if yourselves need no repentance,
Before you pass the bitter sentence!
And ere you judge your brother, first
Remember that yourselves are dust!
But if your conscience tells you then
That your own heart is free from sin –
Cry, with the Pharisee, 'Thank God!
I am not like that wicked clod!'

But to our story of this queer boy
Thady the drunken, devil-may-care boy!
'Twas Christmas Eve – the gale was high –
The snow-clouds swept along the sky;
The flaky drift was whirling down,
Like flying feathers thro' the town.
The tradesman chatted o'er his 'drop',
The Merchant closed his vacant shop
Where, all day long, the busy crowd
Bought Christmas fare, with tumult loud.
The Grocer scored the day's amounts,
The Butcher conn'd his fat accounts;
The Farmer left the noisy mart,

With heavy purse and lighten'd heart.
In every pane the Christmas light
Gave welcome to the holy night;
In every house the holly green
Around the wreathed walls was seen;
The Christmas blocks of oak entire,
Blaz'd, hiss'd and crackled in the fire;
And sounds of joy from every dwelling,
Upon the snowy blast came swelling.

The flying week, now past and gone,
Saw Thady earn two pounds one!
His good employer paid it down,
And warn'd him to refrain from town;
And banned the devilment of drinking,
But Thady scorned his sober thinking;
He fobb'd the coin, with spirit light,
To home and master bade good-night,
And, like a pirate-frigate cruising,
Steer'd to the crowded City, boozing!

The sweet-toned bells of Mary's tower,
Proclaim'd the Saviour's natal hour!
And many an eye with pleasure glisten'd!
And many an ear with rapture listen'd!
The gather'd crowd of charm'd people
Dispersed from gazing at the steeple;
The homeward tread of parting feet,
Died on the echoes of the street;
For Johnny Connell, that dreaded man,
With his wild-raking Garryowen clan,
Clear'd the streets and smash'd each lamp,
And made the watchmen all decamp!

At half-past one the town was silent,
Except a row rais'd in the Island,
Where Thady – foe to sober thinking –
With comrade boys sat gaily drinking!
A table with a pack of cards
Stood in the midst of four blackguards,
Who, with the bumper-draught elated,

Dash'd down their trumps, and swore, and cheated!
Four pints, the fruit of their last game,
White-foaming, to the table came;
They drank, and dealt the cards about,
And Thady brought 'fifteen wheel out'!
Again the deal was Jack Fitzsimon's,
He turned them up, and trumps were diamonds;
The ace was laid by Billy Mara,
And beat with five by Tom O'Hara;
The queen was quickly laid by Thady,
Jack threw the king and douced the lady!
Bill jink'd the game and cried out, 'Waiter!
Bring in the round, before 'tis later!'
The draughts came foaming from the barrel;
The sport soon ended in a quarrel; –
Jack flung a pint at Tom O'Hara,
And Thady levell'd Billy Mara;
The cards flew round in every quarter,
The earthen floor grew drunk with porter;
The landlord ran to call the Watch,
With oaths half Irish and half Scotch.
The Watch came to the scene of battle,
Proclaiming peace, with sounding wattle;
The combatants were soon arrested,
But Thady got off unmolested.

The night was stormy, cold and late,
No human form was in the street;
The virgin snow lay on the highways,
And chok'd up alleys, lanes, and byways.
The North still pout'd its frigid store,
The clouds look'd black and threaten'd more;
The sky was starless, moonless, all
Above the silent world's white pall.
The driving sleet-shower hiss'd aloud –
The distant forest roar'd and bow'd;
But Thady felt no hail nor sleet,
As home he reel'd thro' Castle-street.
The whistling squall was beating on
The batter'd towers of old King John,

Which guarded once, in warlike state,
The hostile pass of Thomond-gate.
The blinding showers, like silvery balls,
Rustled against the ancient walls,
As if determined to subdue
What William's guns had failed to do!
Old Munchin's trees, from roots to heads,
Were rocking in their churchyard beds;
The hoary tombs were wrapt in snow,
The angry Shannon roar'd below.
Thade reel'd along, in slow rotation,
The greatest man in Erin's nation;
Now darting forward, like a pike,
With upraised fist in act to strike;
Now wheeling backward, with the wind,
And half to stand or fall inclined;
Now sidelong, 'mid the pelting showers,
He stumbled near the tall round towers:
With nodding head and zig-zag feet,
He gained the centre of the street;
And, giddy as a summer-midge,
Went staggering towards old Thomond Bridge,
Whose fourteen arches braved so clever,
Six hundred years, the rapid river;
And seem'd, in sooth, a noble picture
Of ancient Irish architecture.

But here the startled Muse must linger,
With tearful eye and pointed finger
To that dark river once the bed
Of Limerick's brave defenders dead –
There half the glorious hope she cherished,
In one sad hour, deluded, perish'd;
The fatal draw-bridge open'd wide,
And gave the warriors to the tide;
The flood received each foremost man,
The rear still madly pressing on;
'Til all the glory of the brave
Was buried in the whirling wave;

And heroes' frames – a bloodless slaughter –
Chok'd up the deep and struggling water.

Now Thady ne'er indulged a thought
How Limerick's heroes fell or fought;
This night he was in no position
For scripture, history, or tradition.
His thoughts were on the Bishop's Lady –
The first tall arch he'd cross'd already;
He paused upon the haunted ground,
The barrier of her midnight round.
Along the Bridge-way, dark and narrow,
He peer'd – while terror drove its arrow,
Cold as the keen blast of October,
Thro' all his frame and made him sober.
Awhile he stood in doubt suspended,
Still to push forward he intended;
When, lo! just as his fears released him,
Up came the angry ghost and seized him!
Ah, Thady! you are done! – Alas!
The Priest's prediction comes to pass –
If you escape this demon's clutch,
The devil himself is not your match!

He saw her face grim, large and pale,
Her red eyes sparkled through her veil;
Her scarlet cloak – half immaterial –
Flew wildly round her person aerial.
With oaths, he tried to grasp her form,
'Twere easier far to catch a storm;
Before his eyes she held him there,
His hands felt nothing more than air;
Her grasp press'd on him cold as steel;
He saw her form but could not feel;
He tried not, tho' his brain was dizzy,
To kiss her, as he kissed Miss Lizzy,
But pray'd to heaven for help sincere –
The first time e'er he said a prayer.

'Twas vain – the Spirit, in her fury,
To do her work was in a hurry;
And, rising, with a whirlwind strength,
Hurl'd him o'er the battlement.
Splash went poor Thady in the torrent,
And roll'd along the rapid current,
Towards Curragour's mad-roaring Fall
The billows tost him, like a ball;
And who dare say, that saw him sinking,
But 'twas his last full round of drinking?
Yet, no – against the river's might
He made a long and gallant fight;
That stream in which he learned to swim,
Shall be no watery grave to him!
Near, and more near he heard the roar
Of rock-impeded Curragour,
Whose torrents, in their headlong sway,
Raged mad as lions for their prey!
Above the Fall he spied afloat
Some object, like an anchor'd boat,
To this, with furious grasp, he clung,
And from the tide his limbs upswung.
Half-frozen in the stern he lay,
Until the holy light of day
Brought forth some kind assisting hand
To row poor Thady to the strand.
'Mid gazing crowds, he left the shore
Well sober'd, and got drunk no more!
And in the whole wide parish round,
A better Christian was not found;
He loved his God and served his neighbour,
And earn'd his bread by honest labour.

Thady, with all his faults, stood bravely by my side when I had the honour of encountering for the first time, at a conference of librarians in Galway city, the renowned Robert Herbert, scholar and historian, and then, and until his death, librarian for Limerick city. Robert had written for *The Limerick Leader* a series of articles on the worthies of

Thomond, which were afterwards collected into a book. And one of those worthies was, most certainly, Michael Hogan, the Bard of Thomond, who wrote about poor Thady and about a lot more in his *Lays and Legends of Thomond*, a formidable volume that first appeared in the Fenian Year of 1867. But the volume that I have just stolen Thady from is a new, select and complete edition published in Limerick city in 1924.

Which reminds me. A distinguished citizen of Limerick, who was also a friend of Robert Herbert, said to me not so long ago: 'A Kiely from Bruff can do no wrong.'

We were standing halfway between the gates of Leinster House and the gate of the National Library.

The point in the remark was that my grandfather came from Bruff. Down in that green and pleasant land they have long memories.

And here is a pleasant memory from that Limerick land. This poem by Jerome Flood, a man from west Cork, I take from David Marcus's book-page in *The Irish Press* for 17 January 1981:

JOHNNY IN KILLALOE

Let me die young or thrive and bloom in Killaloe
And drowse on the bridge, all day, in summer weather
With nothing at all on my mind but a choice of drinks:
'What'll it be today, Johnny, whiskey or Guinness?'
All the rest of my long days, until death comes.

In rain or sun, even here in haunted Killaloe,
I would never remember for long the Danes or the Monks,
Not even Cromwell the whoreson, Collins or Owen Roe
Nor other men whose names were cursed or blessed
From Cork to Derry, Aughrim to Vinegar Hill.

With a breeze I would skim under sail on Lough Derg,
Or stroll at my ease through Owney & Arrah
Or lie in some scented meadow above Portroe

With nothing much on my mind but names for islands
Dim on the hazy Lough – islands in the Sea of China.

The girls I'd court would be Clare girls, mostly,
Farmers' daughters, soft-eyed, supple and willing
With nothing averse in the heart to love under hedges,
Eager to comfort a single man with no harm in him,
And take a chance, at times, at more than kissing.

For a change, I would cross the long bridge to Ballina
And stretch my length by the Graves of the Leinstermen,
Sharing the skyward joy of the enraptured lark
And wish it is I were the grass-hidden hopper
Frittering the sunlit hour away, near my left hand.

From a choice of mansions in the woods of Leinster
Or a castle in Ulster with three avenue-gates
With no regrets in my mind I would turn
And choose Killaloe for the fine delights of my days
All the rest of my long days, until death comes.

And now that I think of it, 'twas another Kerryman, and
one of the greatest, who first gave me the words of that
wildest of all (almost) Limerick songs: 'The Limerick Rake'.

I'm talking now of Sigerson Clifford, not only in himself
a composer of poems and ballads, but a great and scholarly
authority on the songs sung here and there in Munster for
many years. I take the words of 'The Limerick Rake' from
Sigerson's *Book of Irish Recitations*, published by Bentee
Books (Dun Laoire: 1960).

THE LIMERICK RAKE

I am a young fellow, as wild as a goat,
In Castletown Conyers I'm also well-known,
In Newcastle West I spent many a note
With Nellie and Judy and Mary.
My father abused me for being such a rake
And wasting my time in such frolicking ways.
But I ne'er could forget the kind nature of Kate.
And we'll leave the old world as we find it.

From Connacht to Munster

My parents had reared me to shake and to mow,
To plough and to harrow, to reap and to sow.
But my heart being too airy to drop it so low
I set out on a high speculation.
On paper and parchment they taught me to write,
In Euclid and grammar they opened my eyes,
And in multiplication, in truth, I was bright.
And we'll leave the old world as we find it.

If I chance for to go to the town of Rathkeale
The girls all around me do flock on the Square.
Some to give me a bottle, and others sweet cakes
To treat me, unknown to their parents.
There is one from Askeaton and one from the Pike,
Another from Ards my heart has beguiled,
Though being from the mountains her stockings are white.
And we'll leave the old world as we find it.

To quarrel for riches I ne'er was inclined
For the greatest of misers must leave them behind.
I'll purchase a cow that will never run dry
And I'll milk her by twisting her horn.
John Damer of Shronel had plenty of gold,
And Devonshire's treasure is twenty times more,
But he's laid on his back among nettles and stones.
And we'll leave the old world as we find it.

This cow can be milked without clover or grass
For she's pampered with corn, good barley and hops.
She's warm and stout, and she's free in her paps,
And she'll milk without spancel or halter.
The man that will drink it will cock his caubeen,
And if anyone cough there'll be wigs on the geen,
And the feeble old hags will get supple and free.
And we'll leave the old world as we find it.

If I chance for to go to the market of Croom,
With a cock in my hat and my pipes in full tune,
I am welcome at once, and brought up to a room
Where Bacchus is sporting with Venus.
There's Peggy and Jane from the town of Bruree,
And Biddy from Bruff, and we all on the spree.

Such a combing of locks as there is about me.
And we'll leave the old world as we find it.

There's some says I'm foolish and more says I'm wise,
But being fond of the women I think is no crime,
For the son of King David had ten hundred wives
And his wisdom was highly recorded.
I'll till a good garden and live at my ease,
And each woman and child can partake of the same,
If there's war in the cabins theirselves they may blame,
And we'll leave the old world as we find it.

And now for the future, I mean to be wise
And I'll send for the women that acted so kind,
And I'll marry them all on the morrow, by-and-by,
If the clergy agree to the bargain.
And when I'm on my back, and my soul has no ache,
These women will crowd for to cry at my wake.
And their sons and their daughters will offer their prayers
To the Lord for the soul of their father.

What genius of a rural pedagogue, I wonder, composed that marvellous song. Reread it, instanter, or re-sing it, and meditate on the classical style, the philosophy, and the profound consideration of the Four Last, or First, Things.

And the movement and the rhythm set going in my head a lovely song which, as far as I can remember, was first mentioned to me by that wonderful woman and singer, Delia Murphy:

THE LAMBS ON THE GREEN HILLS

The lambs on the green hills stood gazing at me,
And many strawberries grow round the salt sea,
And many strawberries grow round the salt sea,
And many a ship sails the ocean.

The bride and bride's party to church they did go,
The bride she rode foremost, she bears the best show,
But I followed after with my heart full of woe
For to see my love wed to another.

The first place I saw her was on the church stand,
Golden rings on her finger and her love by the hand.
Says I: 'My wee lassie, I will be the man
Although you are wed to another.'

The next place I saw her was on the way home,
I ran on before her, not knowing where to roam.
Says I: 'My wee lassie, I'll be by your side
Although you are wed to another.'

'Stop stop,' says the groomsman, 'till I speak a word,
'Will you venture your life on the point of my sword?
For courting so slowly you've lost this fair maid,
So begone for you'll never enjoy her.'

Oh come, make my grave then both large, wide and deep,
And sprinkle it over with flowers so sweet,
And lay me down in it to take my last sleep,
For that's the best way to forget her.

And moving to the same rhythm, more or less, I recall this old fragment of a mummer's song, by Padraic Colum. It appeared first, as far as I know, in his novel *Castle Conquer*. Which novel, he once told me, he did not like and I modestly begged to differ.

Howandever: the lively lines were repeated in a centenary volume in honour of Colum, *The Poet's Circuits* (Dolmen Press 1981), for which I was privileged to write the introduction.

The mummers come dancing to the door, with designs, clearly not villainous, on the daughter of the house. And they are rousingly answered:

For a bride you have come! Is it with a full score
Of rake-hell rapscallions you'd fill up my door,
With a drum to your tail and a fiddle before,
And a bag-piper playing all through ye?

My faith! Do you think that a shy little maid
Would lift up her head before such a brigade,

When an arm round her waist would make her afraid?
By my hand! She has gone from my keeping.

Through the gap in the hedges away she has run;
Like the partridge across the wide stubble she's gone,
And here I am, here I am, here I'm alone
With no daughter to give any comer!

Well, here she is back! I declare she has come
Like the cat to the cradle, and Nance she's at home:
O my love, would you go to the bleak hills of Crome,
Where nor manners nor mirth are in fashion?

O say not you'll go! That you'll never embark
From a plentiful house where you prize every spark,
Where there's milk in the crock and meal in the ark,
And a pair of fat ducks for the roasting!

Oh, mother sell all that you have to your name,
To give me a dowry to equal my fame –
Sell the cow, and the sow, and the gander that's lame,
And the sack of black wool in the corner!

And my good-will I'll leave to our Babe that stays here,
May she leave the bog-bottoms within the half-year,
Where the rushes are high and the curlews call near,
And the crows on the hill they are lonely.

With rake-hell young fellows my Babe will not go,
Nor look from her dormer on faction below,
From up where the picture and looking-glass show
That elegance holds and good order!

Maureen Jolliffe in her *The Third Book of Irish Ballads* (Mercier 1970) reminds us that Michael Hogan, the Bard of Thomond (1832–90), was a wheelwright who upheld the Irish tradition of artisan ballad-makers, in company with Thomas W. Condon, a locksmith of Waterford, John 'de Jean' Frazer, a cabinet-maker of Birr, Francis Davis, 'The Belfast Man', a weaver, and a man from Ballincollig, Co. Cork. And more. A sedentary occupation was a great help to the Muse.

But on another page of her book Maureen Jolliffe gives us Michael Scanlan, a Limerick man, who wrote one of the two greatest Fenian songs. The other was written by Peadar Cearnaigh.

It was said that men were sent to jail for singing Scanlan's song and Scanlan (1836–1900) in exile in the States used to worry about that. (He also wrote one of my mother's favourite songs, 'The Jackets Green'.)

THE BOLD FENIAN MEN

See who come over the red-blossomed heather,
Their green banners kissing the pure mountain air,
Head erect, eyes to front, stepping proudly together,
Sure freedom sits throned on each proud spirit there.
Down the hill twining,
Their blessed steel shining,
Like rivers of beauty that flow from each glen,
From mountain and valley,
'Tis Liberty's rally –
Out and make way for the Bold Fenian Men.

Our prayers and our tears have been scoffed and derided,
They've shut out God's sunlight from spirit and mind;
Our foes were united and we were divided,
We met and they scattered our ranks to the wind;
But once more returning,
Within our veins burning
The fires that illumined dark Aherlow Glen,
We raise the cry anew,
Slogan of Conn and Hugh –
Out and make way for the Bold Fenian Men!

Up for the cause, then, fling forth our green banners,
From the East to the West, from the South to the North –
Irish land, Irish men, Irish mirth, Irish manners –
From the mansion and cot let the slogan go forth.
Sons of old Ireland now,
Love you our sireland now?
Come from the kirk, or the chapel or glen;

195

Down with the faction old,
Concert and action bold,
This is the creed of the Bold Fenian Men!

We've men from the Nore, from the Suir and the Shannon,
Let the tyrants come forth, we'll bring force against force,
Our pen is the sword and our voice is the cannon,
Rifle for rifle and horse against horse,
We've made the false Saxon yield
Many a red battlefield:
God on our side, we will triumph again;
Pay them back woe for woe,
Give them back blow for blow –
Out and make way for the Bold Fenian Men!

Side by side for the cause have our forefathers battled,
When our hills never echoed the tread of a slave;
In many a field where the leaden hail rattled,
Through the red gap of glory they marched to the grave.
And those who inherit
Their name and their spirit,
Will march 'neath the banners of Liberty then;
All who love foreign law –
Native or Sasanach –
Must out and make way for the Bold Fenian Men.

But appealing once again to the ghost of James Clarence
Mangan ... Let him recall us to the great glory of the ancient
Limerick land:

KINCORA
[*from the Irish*]

Oh, where, Kincora! is Brian the Great?
And where is the beauty that once was thine?
Oh, where are the princes and nobles that sate
At the feast in thy halls, and drank the red wine?
Where, oh, Kincora?

Oh, where, Kincora! are thy valorous lords?
Oh, whither, thou Hospitable! are they gone?

196

From Connacht to Munster

Oh, where are the Dalcassians of the Golden Swords?
And where are the warriors Brian led on?
Where, oh, Kincora?

And where is Murrough, the descendant of kings –
The defeater of a hundred – the daringly brave –
Who set but slight store by jewels and rings –
Who swam down the torrent and laughed at its wave?
Where, oh, Kincora?

And where is Donogh, King Brian's worthy son?
And where is Conaing, the Beautiful Chief?
And Kian, and Corc? Alas! they are gone –
They have left me this night alone with my grief,
Left me, Kincora!

And where are the chiefs with whom Brian went forth,
The ne'er vanquished son of Evin the Brave,
The great King of Onaght, renowned for his worth,
And the hosts of Baskinn, from the western wave?
Where, oh, Kincora?

Oh, where is Duvlann of the Swift-footed Steeds?
And where is Kian, who is son of Molloy?
And where is King Lonergan, the fame of whose deeds
In the red battle-field no time can destroy?
Where, oh, Kincora?

And where is that youth of majestic height,
The faith-keeping Prince of the Scots? – Even he,
As wide as his fame was, as great as was his might,
Was tributary, oh, Kincora, to thee!
Thee, oh, Kincora!

They are gone, those heroes of royal birth
Who plundered no churches, and broke no trust,
'Tis weary for me to be living on earth
When they, oh, Kincora, lie low in the dust!
Low, oh, Kincora!

Oh, never again will Princes appear,
To rival the Dalcassians of the Cleaving Swords!
I can never dream of meeting afar or anear,

In the east or the west, such heroes and lords!
Never, Kincora!

Oh, dear are the images my memory calls up
Of Brian Boru! – how he never would miss
To give me at the banquet the first bright cup!
Ah! why did he heap on me honour like this?
Why, oh, Kincora?

I am Mac Liag, and my home is on the Lake;
Thither often, to that palace whose beauty is fled,
Came Brian to ask me, and I went for his sake.
Oh, my grief! that I should live, and Brian be dead!
Dead, oh, Kincora!

And from Limerick on, by way of Con Houlihan's Castleisland, into the World of the Southwest. Where to begin? Where to end? Or, perhaps, where to pause for breath. For in those sublime places there never is an end to poems and ballads.

And what place could be more sublime than St Finnbarr's deep, strange glen:

GOUGAUNE BARRA

There is a green island in lone Gougaune Barra,
Where Allua of songs rushes forth like an arrow;
In deep-valleyed Desmond – a thousand wild fountains
Come down to that lake, from their home in the mountains.
There grows the wild ash, and a time-stricken willow
Looks chidingly down on the mirth of the billow;
As, like some gay child, that sad monitor scorning,
It lightly laughs back to the laugh of the morning.

And its zone of dark hills – O to see them all brightening,
When the tempest flings out its red banner of lightning,
And the waters rush down, 'mid the thunder's deep rattle,
Like clans from their hills at the voice of the battle;
And brightly the fire-crested billows are gleaming,
And wildly from Mullagh the eagles are screaming.

From Connacht to Munster

O where is the dwelling in valley or highland,
So meet for a bard as this lone little island?

How oft when the summer sun rested on Clara,
And lit the dark heath on the hills of Ivera,
Have I sought thee, sweet spot, from my home by the ocean,
And trod all thy wilds with a minstrel's devotion,
And thought of thy bards, when assembling together,
In the cleft of thy rocks, or the depth of thy heather,
They fled from the Saxon's dark bondage and slaughter,
And waked their last song by the rush of thy water?

High sons of the lyre, O how proud was the feeling!
To think while alone through that solitude stealing,
Though loftier Minstrels green Erin can number,
I only awoke your wild harp from its slumber,
And mingled once more with the voice of those fountains
The songs even echo forgot on her mountains;
And gleaned each grey legend that darkly was sleeping
Where the mist and the rain o'er their beauty were creeping!

Least bard of the hills! were it mine to inherit
The fire of thy harp, and the wing of thy spirit,
With the wrongs which like thee to our country have bound me,
Did your mantle of song fling its radiance around me,
Still, still in those wilds might young Liberty rally,
And send her strong shout over mountain and valley,
The star of the west might yet rise in its glory,
And the land that was darkest be brightest in story.

I too shall be gone; – but my name shall be spoken
When Erin awakes, and her fetters are broken;
Some Minstrel will come, in the summer eve's gleaming,
When Freedom's young light on his spirit is beaming,
And bend o'er my grave with a tear of emotion,
Where calm Avon-Bwee seeks the kisses of ocean,
Or plant a wild wreath, from the banks of that river,
O'er the heart and the harp that are sleeping for ever.

[J.J. Callanan]

Jeremiah Joseph Callanan, a poet and a lonely sort of a man, was born in Cork in 1795 and died in Lisbon in 1829. He had gone to Lisbon looking for health in a sunnier climate than Ireland could provide. He had been a student in Maynooth until ill-health drove him out. Then he was in TCD for two years and left for the same reason.

Then, through the influence of that eccentric friend of W.M. Thackeray, the Corkonian Dr William Maginn, of the 'Homeric Ballads' (and of course Mangan's 'the gulf and grave of Maginn and Burns'), Callanan became a contributor to the famous *Blackwood's Magazine* in London. But Callanan stayed at home and wandered Ireland, listening to legends and songs, and even translating some of them. Then he rested for a while on the island of Inchidony and wrote a poem, 'The Recluse of Inchidony', which the young Mr Yeats, later on, did not exactly praise.

Poor Callanan went off to Lisbon, for the sake of his health and to work as a tutor to the family of an Irish gentleman. He died there.

He did write well about the sacred coomb of Gougane Barra. And being himself a lonely sort of man he was receptive to that most lonely song: 'Sé dubhach é mo chás'.

Whoever wrote it captured agonizingly the loneliness of an unfortunate man on the eve of his hanging in the jail of Clonmel. And Callanan dressed it up in suitable mourning clothes in the English:

THE CONVICT OF CLONMEL

How hard is my fortune,
And vain my repining!
The strong rope of Fate
For this young neck is twining.
My strength is departed,
My cheek sunk and sallow,
While I languish in chains
In the jail of Cluanmeala.

No boy in the village
Was ever yet milder,
I'd play with a child
And my sport would be wilder.
I'd dance without tiring
From morning till even,
And my goal-ball I'd strike
To the lightning of Heaven.

At my bed-foot decaying,
My hurlbat is lying,
Through the boys of the village
My goal-ball is flying.
My horse, among the neighbours,
Neglected may fallow,
While I pine in my chains
In the jail of Cluanmeala.

Next Sunday the patron
At home will be keeping,
And the young, active hurlers
The field will be sweeping.
With the dance of fair maidens
The evening they'll hallow,
While this heart, once so warm,
Will be cold in Cluanmeala.

It is a happy memory of mine that it was a talk I had one
day with Luke Kelly of the Dubliners that made Luke
decide to record 'The Convict of Clonmel'. Which, as most
of us know, he did to perfection. And Luke had also decided
to record Callanan's 'The Outlaw of Loch Lene'. But, alas,
death claimed him before that was accomplished. The fourth
and last verse Luke particularly fancied. As who wouldn't?

O many a day have I made good ale in the glen,
That came not of stream or malt – like the brewing of men.
My bed was the ground; my roof, the greenwood above,
And the wealth that I sought one far kind glance from my love.

Alas! on that night when the horses I drove from the field,
That I was not near from terror my angel to shield,
She stretched forth her arms, – her mantle she flung to the wind,
And swam o'er Loch Lene, her outlawed lover to find.

O would that a freezing sleet-winged tempest did sweep,
And I and my love were alone, far off on the deep:
I'd ask not a ship, or a bark, or pinnace, to save –
With her hand round my waist, I'd fear not the wind or the wave.

'Tis down by the lake where the wild tree fringes its sides,
The maid of my heart, the fair one of heaven resides; –
I think as at eve she wanders its mazes along,
The birds go to sleep by the sweet wild twist of her song.

And then back, for a while, to Gougane Barra and some memories, out of our own time, that that sacred name inevitably provokes. There is Seán Ó Faoláin's story 'The Silence of the Valley'. Then there is the story of Eric Cross, the good Englishman, wandering the roads of Ireland with a horse and caravan, the purchase of which, in Dublin, he had been advised by the novelist Francis MacManus. When Eric got to Gougane Barra whom should he meet but the renowned tailor and his wife. And Cross looked at them and listened to them, and loved them, and wrote a lovely book about them, for which Frank O'Connor wrote the introduction.

The story of the banning of that book by the idiotic book-censorship of the time is well known. And Seamus Murphy, the sculptor, who did a fine head of the Tailor, told me that the nasty hullabaloo about the book broke the Tailor's heart and hastened his end. To his memory and that of other merry men who are gone let's have a few lively verses from Frank O'Connor. Book-censorship is now, mercifully, extinct, so O'Connor's recall of the three old brothers can't get this book banned. We hope.

From Connacht to Munster

While some goes dancing reels and some
Goes stuttering love in ditches,
The three old brothers rise from bed,
And moan, and pin their breeches.
And one says, 'I can sleep no more,
I'd liefer far go weeping,
For how can honest men lie still
When brats can spoil their sleeping?'

And blind Tom says, that's eighty years,
'If I was ten years younger
I'd take a stick and welt their rumps
And gall their gamest runner.'
Then James the youngest cries, 'Praise God,
We have outlived our passion!'
And by their fire of roots all three
Praise God after a fashion.

Says James, 'I loved, when I was young,
A lass of one and twenty,
That had the grace of all the queens
And broke men's hearts in plenty;
But now the girl's a gammy crone,
With no soft sides or bosom,
And all the ones she kist, abed
Where the fat maggot chews 'em.
And though she had not kiss for me,
And though myself is older,
And though my thighs are cold to-night,
Their thighs, I think, are colder.'

And Blind Tom says, 'I knew a man
A girl refused for lover
Worked in America forty years
And heaped copper on copper;
And came back all across the foam,
Dressed up in silks and satins,
And watched for her from dawn to dark,
And from Compline to Matins;
And when she passed him in her shawl,

He bust his sides with laughing,
And went back happy to the West,
And heeded no man's scoffing.
And Christ,' moans Tom, 'if I'd his luck
I'd not mind cold nor coughing.'
Then Patcheen says, 'My lot's a lot
All men on earth might envy,
That saw the girl I could not get
Nurse an untimely baby.'

And all three say, 'Dear heart! Dear heart!'
And James the youngest mutters,
'Praise God we have outlived our griefs
And not fell foul like others,
Like Paris and the Grecian chiefs
And the three Ulster brothers!'

And in the mood promoted by O'Connor's celebration of that unholy trinity we may happily journey back in time to join Richard Alfred Milliken in the groves of Blarney. Milliken (as my old friend Halliday Sparling tells me) was born in Castlemartyr, County Cork, in 1767, and died in 1816. And, even in Sparling's time, poor Milliken was remembered only as the author of this: 'The Groves of Blarney'. Which, even at that, was only a burlesque on, or a caricature of, the poem about Castlehyde written, around 1790, by Barrett the Weaver. Men of sedentary occupations always were, as we may have noticed, great men for the writing. Milliken, alas, has a blot on his scutcheon. He was, in 1798, one of the Yeos and was commended, by whoever ran the show, for doing his job very well. Regardless of which, and, God help us all, it was a long time ago, let's hear him on 'The Groves of Blarney':

The groves of Blarney they look so charming,
Down by the purling of sweet, silent streams,
Being banked with posies there spontaneous growing
Planted in order by the sweet rock close.
'Tis there's the daisy and the sweet carnation,

The blooming pink and the rose so fair,
The daffodowndilly, likewise the lily,
All flowers that scent the sweet, fragrant air.

'Tis Lady Jeffers that owns this station;
Like Alexander, or Queen Helen fair,
There's no commander in all the nation,
For emulation, can with her compare.
Such walls surround her, that no nine-pounder
Could dare to plunder her place of strength;
But Oliver Cromwell her he did pommel,
And made a breach in her battlement.

There's gravel walks there for speculation
And conversation in sweet solitude.
'Tis there the lover may hear the dove, or
The gentle plover in the afternoon;
And if a lady would be so engaging
As to walk alone in those shady bowers,
'Tis there the courtier he may transport her
Into some fort, or all under ground.

For 'tis there's a cave where no daylight enters,
But cats and badgers are for ever bred;
Being mossed by nature, that makes it sweeter
Than a coach-and-six or a feather bed.
'Tis there the lake is, well stored with perches,
And comely eels in the verdant mud;
Besides the leeches, and groves of beeches,
Standing in order for to guard the flood.

There's statues gracing this noble place in –
All heathen gods and nymphs so fair;
Bold Neptune, Plutarch, and Nicodemus,
All standing naked in the open air!
So now to finish this brave narration,
Which my poor genii could not entwine;
But were I Homer, or Nebuchadnezzar,
'Tis in every feature I would make it shine.

Francis Sylvester Mahony (Father Prout) had, inevitably, his own version, in several languages, of that song. Here is Prout's final verse:

There is a boat on the lake to float on,
And lots of beauties which I can't entwine.
But were I a preacher, or classic teacher,
In every feature I'd make 'em shine.
There is a stone that whoever kisses
O! He never misses to grow eloquent.
'Tis he may clamber to a lady's chamber
Or become a Member of Parliament.
A clever spouter he'll soon turn out, or
An Out-and-Outer to be let alone.
Don't hope to hinder him or to bewilder him
Sure he's a pilgrim from the Blarney Stone.

Father Prout almost always had the last word. But now that we are in the neighbourhood we are compelled (or it is incumbent on us - or coin any phrase that pleases you) to listen to the voice of Barrett the Weaver and what he had to say about Castle Hyde:

As I roved out on a summer's morning,
Down by the banks of the Blackwater side,
To view the groves and the meadows charming,
And the pleasant gardens of Castle Hyde.
'Tis there you'd hear the thrushes warbling,
The dove and partridge I now describe,
And lambkins sporting every morning,
All to adorn sweet Castle Hyde.

There are fine walks in those pleasant gardens
And seats most charming in shady bowers,
The gladiator, who is bold and daring,
Each night and morning to watch the flowers.
There's a road for service, in this fine arbour,
Where nobles in their coaches ride
To view the groves and pleasant gardens
That front the palace of Castle Hyde.

If noble princes from foreign places
Should chance to sail to the Irish shore,
'Tis in this valley they should be feasted

Where often heroes had been before.
The wholesome air of this habitation
Would recreate your heart with pride,
There is no valley throughout this nation
In beauty equal to Castle Hyde.

There are fine horses and staff-fed oxen,
A den for foxes to play and hide,
Fine mares for breeding, and foreign sheep
With snowy fleeces in Castle Hyde.
The grand improvements there would amuse you
The trees are drooping with fruits of all kinds,
The bees perfuming the fields with music
Which yields more beauty to Castle Hyde.

The richest groves throughout this nation
In fine plantations you will see there,
The rose, the tulip and the sweet carnation
All vying with the lily fair.
The buck and doe, the fox and eagle,
They skip and play by the riverside,
The trout and salmon are always sporting
In the crystal waters of Castle Hyde.

I roved from Blarney to Castle Arney,
From Thomastown to Doneraile,
And Killishannock that joins Rathcormack,
Besides Killarney and Abbeyfeale.
The flowing Nore, the rapid Boyne,
The river Shannon and the pleasant Clyde,
But in all my ranging and serenading
I saw none to equal sweet Castle Hyde.

For a sedentary and a humble man, Barrett the Weaver had a great vision of glory, and he saw that Castle Hyde had distinct resemblances to a place called Eden, also famous in folklore. But that was the way with the makers of ballads long ago; one place on earth must surpass all others. Wasn't there a later rhymester who made an old man say:

The priests have got a book that says
But for Adam's sin,
Eden's grandson would be there
And I there, within ...

Howandever! As I often say.

But pause awhile.

Which reminds me. There was and old parish priest once, away up in the Sperrin Mountains, who, when he was walking around the church and reading out for the mountain faithful the stories and prayers relating to the Via Crucis, used to say at regular intervals: Pause awhile.

This was why.

The way the old prayer-books had it (and perhaps the new ones may still have it) was: first, a little visual picture of the event of that station; what the Ignatian method of prayers would call a Composition of Place. Then followed an out-loud prayer. But in between was simply printed: Pause Awhile.

Meaning: you were to meditate a bit on what you had seen, or on what had been described to you: 'Those barbarians fastened him with nails etc.'

So, here and now, pause awhile and rest. For this is a long and intricate road round Ireland. And that mention of the Sperrin Mountains brings me out of my meditation to hear the soft voice of an old school-friend of mine who still, and happily, survives up in those places. He is, to my ears, singing his favourite song, and in his singing uniting Ireland in a most moving way: from O'Neill's Sperrins to the deaf glens of Munster. For his favourite song was John Todhunter's 'Aghadoe':

From Connacht to Munster

There's a glade in Aghadoe, Aghadoe, Aghadoe,
There's a green and silent glade in Aghadoe,
Where we met, my love and I, love's fair planet in the sky,
O'er that sweet and silent glade in Aghadoe.

There's a glen in Aghadoe, Aghadoe, Aghadoe,
There's a deep and secret glen in Aghadoe,
Where I hid him from the eyes of the red-coats and their spies,
That year the trouble came to Aghadoe.

Oh! my curse on one black heart in Aghadoe, Aghadoe,
On Shaun Dhuv, my mother's son, in Aghadoe!
When your throat fries in hell's drouth, salt the flame be in your mouth,
For the treachery you did in Aghadoe!

For they tracked me to that glen in Aghadoe, Aghadoe,
When the price was on his head in Aghadoe,
O'er the mountain, by the wood, as I stole to him with food,
Where in hiding lone he lay in Aghadoe.

But they never took him living in Aghadoe, Aghadoe,
With the bullets in his heart in Aghadoe,
There he lay – the head my breast feels the warmth of, where 'twould rest,
Gone, to win the traitor's gold, from Aghadoe!

I walked to Mallow town from Aghadoe, Aghadoe,
Brought his head from the gaol's gate to Aghadoe,
Then I covered him with fern, and I piled him on the cairn,
Like an Irish king he sleeps in Aghadoe.

Oh! to creep into that cairn in Aghadoe, Aghadoe!
There to rest upon his breast in Aghadoe,
Sure your dog for you could die with no truer heart than I,
Your own love, cold on your cairn, in Aghadoe.

V

And Back to Tyrrellspass

What was it just now that halted my career on my crazy road round Ireland and set me stamping on the roadside grass to find firm footing, and a faint booming echo? It was the glimmer of old timber, hidden and smothered by the grass, but once a bright and shining platform where the young people of the neighbourhood met to dance: with or without proper parental or clerical supervision.

And a poem or a song came back to me and set me off back north on a tangent to a place called Callenberg, a close neighbour of Patrick Kavanagh's Inniskeen.

Here's the poem or song. You may dance to it:

THE DECK BESIDE THE ROAD

You may talk about your city life and of the latest play,
And while you are enjoying them you feel both light and gay,
I care not for your dramas nor for your fancy balls,
Give me the homely gathering where the Irish tweeds and shawls
Are sported down in Rosslough, not far from my abode,
By the buachaills and the cáilins on the Deck beside the Road.

A word of praise for Thomas Kirk, he gave the timber free,
And the joiner Tommy Murray, he left it as you see.
But the Scotsman, Tom Gilmartin, his praise we all echoed,
For the ground, he gave it gratis, for the Deck beside the Road.

And God forbid I would forget our Local Committee,
There is Bernard Owen and Tommy, Joe Nugent and Frank Fee,
These learned men of talents great, made out of rules or code,
Which was enforced most stringent on the Deck beside the Road.

The good priest listened for a while and then he said: he thought
These round dances were an awful curse, and ruin often brought
To maidens young and innocent, of grief a heavy load.
So I can't give my consent to have this Deck beside the Road.

The Committee looked sorrowful, a tear hung from each eye,
When John Garvey to his Reverence he made this quick reply:
'Oh, Father dear, at seven o'clock each lass to her abode
Must go without a sweetheart from the Deck beside the Road.'

'Now John, act to your promise and you'll have my consent.'
With three cheers for the sagart, it's cheerful home they went,
The messengers they were despatched, on bicycles astrode,
To tell the boys and girls about the Deck beside the Road.

And on the Sunday after, what groups assembled there
From Dundalk, Carrick, Crossmaglen, and Louth too sent its share.
James Drumgoole set them in motion, how sweet his music flowed
Across the bogs and rushes from the Deck beside the Road.

John Duffy, the young tailor, danced jigs, aye nine or ten,
Outclassing Grant the Champion from dear old Crossmaglen.
But, on my oath, the Muckler Grant when Sweet Moll Roe he told
He had the widows smiling at the Deck beside the Road.

Now, when the dance is over, see the cáilíns with their pails
Milking the cows upon the hills and in the flowery vales,
And hear them chat about the dance as home they bear their load
Across the stiles and boreens from the Deck beside the Road.

My blessings on each lad and lass who loves an Irish dance,
And my curse upon the men who first commenced the Game of Chance,
For from my trouser-pocket where some shillings bright were stowed
They disappeared last Sunday at the Deck beside the Road.

Now the last dancing-board, or crossroads or roadside
dancing-deck that I remember seeing in all its glory was on
the Boa Island in Lough Erne: and that was sometime in the
1930s. Although I must not forget the Square at the top of
Roquey Rocks in Bundoran where, when the weather was
behaving itself, Irish dancing was, and may still be, ex-
cellently performed.

The commercial dancehall killed such places, with the oddest ally in the old-style clergy who did not like the idea of the open-air dances when the dusk came on and the couples might fade out, when their blood was up, into the fields and hedgerows to do all sorts of sinful deeds. The idea was, in those innocent days, that if the young must dance at all (and the young and quite a few of the old will insist on dancing) then they had better do it in the parish hall and under proper supervision. Improper supervision would be no use at all. And how long is it now since to dance after midnight on one side of the river (or what the E.S.B. left of the river) in Ballyshannon was a sin. But on the other side of the river you could dance until dawn rose and your feet fell off, and your immortal soul not be one bit the worse for wear. Nowadays the College of Cardinals and the Choirs of Angels, all armed with electric guitars, could hardly make their voices heard to supervise or anything else in a discotheque – although their costumes and, perhaps, the angelic hairstyles, could attract admiring attention.

The poets long ago cast an eye on the roadside dancing-decks. And it is most likely that the anonymous author of 'Sé Dubhach é Mo Chas' was thinking of some such place when he wrote the lines that J.J. Callanan upset so well into the English:

> With the dance of fair maidens
> The evening they will hallow,
> While this heart once so warm
> Shall be cold in Cluan Meala.

And John McEnaney, the Bard of Callenberg, in his pursuit of the proper study of mankind and with an occasional dart at justifying the ways of God to man, did write the great poem, or song, which we have just read, or sung.

The Bard of Callenberg, as we have noted, was against gambling because of sad experience. He was also against

drink even if he did like it and caroused a bit. For when he
was inviting friends to come to his wedding reception in
Paddy Kavanagh's village of Inniskeen he promised them
music but warned them severely against he dangers of drink.
Listen to him:

> But if you like sweet music I pray you do come down
> To hear Fiddler Conor Cumiskey and B. Murray of Stonetown.
> We'll treat you to the very best. But your whistle you can't wet
> With whiskey, ale or porter. Too soon you might regret.
> So is you come to Inniskeen you'll return home, I think,
> With a firm resolution to ne'er give way to drink.

He was also against the British Empire and for the gallant
Boers and General de Wet. He was all for love of country
and for love of a girl called the Star of Inniskeen, whom it
would seem that he married, against the opposition of many
fellow bards of *The Donegal Democrat*. And as far as I can
judge by what the scholars would call the internal evidence
of his poems, he was devoted to the then emergent Gaelic
football and the men who played it; and we must remember
that, at a later date, Patrick the Poet kept goal for Inniskeen.

But Pause Awhile, as the old parish-priest used to say
every now and then in the course of the Stations of the
Cross. Pause Awhile and meditate.

Do I hear somebody in the back of the hall saying that (as
did two old retired schoolmasters in the snug of a pub in
Dundalk, and in my hearing) he or she, man, woman or
person, has never heard of the Bard of Callenberg? Well he
walks, alive and singing, into one of the prose fragments of
Patrick Kavanagh that Patrick's brother, Peter, had published
under the title of 'By Night Unstarred'. Patrick wrote: 'Off
in the nearby bog, John the Bard, a notorious character who
spoke only in rhyme, had a visit from his neighbour, Johnny
Longcoat's mother, who hadn't been on speaking terms with

him for more than a year. The Bard, who had been out breaking gravel for the road contractor, limped in on his crutches. As we said, the Bard always spoke in rhyme. Once when he sued this very neighbour he addressed the Court:

> My heart with indignation swells
> As I state my case to Mr Wells:
> Alas! To tell about my bother
> With Johnny Longcoat and his mother ...

And so on. That was how Patrick Kavanagh introduced the Bard and that, I feel, is the way every poet should talk. What's the use of being, or of being called Thomas Kinsella or John Montague or Seamus Heaney if you go about talking prose? Anybody could do that. I could do it myself.

And another Bard, by the name of Scott, wrote in praise of John McEnaney, the Bard of Callenberg:

> From Clogherhead to Castleblayney,
> And from Carrick Town to dear Lough Derg,
> There's none to equal John McEnaney,
> The famous Bard from sweet Callenberg.
> They may talk of Shelley and Paddy Kelly;
> And Alfie Austen who is all put-on,
> Why the great Lord Byron couldn't hold an iron
> To smooth the collar of immortal John.
> Sure Mudguard Kipling is all up the spout.
> And the great Shakespearian he quakes in fear again
> The *Dundalk Democrat* again comes out...

Few poets ever spoke so well, so nobly, about another poet.

The rattle of all those feet bouncing on the Deck beside the Road must have got to my head, and my feet. Nor can I rest now until I'm back to boyhood and meet a circus on the road and on the way to the town. Denis A. McCarthy wrote the lines we need:

And Back to Tyrrellspass

The circus, the circus is coming to town,
With camel and elephant, rider and clown,
With horses and ponies, the best to behold,
And chariots all gleaming with scarlet and gold,
With cages of lions that blink at the light,
And tigers all baring their teeth for a fight,
With banners and flags, all bespangled with stars,
With cowboys and Indians, soldiers and tars,
With jugglers and jumpers, magicians and monkeys,
With richly-dressed knights, fair ladies and flunkeys,
With giants and dwarfs of the widest renown –
The circus, the circus is coming to town.

The circus, the circus is coming to town,
With strange-looking people all brawny and brown,
With athletes and acrobats ready to seize
And soar through the air on the flying trapeze.
With rattle of harness and rumble of wheels,
And bands playing jigs and quick marches and reels,
With torches that flare in the darkness of night,
While all the folks gather to stare at the sight.
With canvas and tent-pegs and guy-ropes and poles,
And children delighted all running in shoals.
The face of a child has no place for a frown
When told that the circus is coming to town.

The circus, the circus is coming to town.
The boys all excitement run up and run down,
Devouring the posters which, everyone knows,
With modesty speaks of the greatest of shows.
And there is much planning oh how to obtain
A ticket to enter the magic domain.
And hope rises high in the heart of each lad
That he may be taken, perhaps, by his dad,
To see all the wonders and feel all the thrills
So lavishly promised, and praised, on the bills
Of all the good news, this good news is the crown
The circus, the circus is coming to town.

The circus, the circus is coming to town.
That call in my memory no noises can drown.

It rings in my heart as when first, long ago,
I saw the big posters announcing the show.
When Bill and myself read on Haggerty's gate
The name which began with the adjective Great,
Then wandered around from one fence to the next,
Just gloating with joy over picture and text.
And so, when I see on the fences today,
The bright-coloured posters their promise display
Of rider and wrestler, of camel and clown,
I'm glad that the circus is coming to town.

Thirty-four years ago I was writing, under the name of Patrick Lagan, a daily column for a revered daily newspaper that, God help us, is no longer with us. What an outrage that *The Irish Press* should no longer be part of our national life.

But thirty-four years ago I was hunting for the words of that old poem about the circus. I remembered reading it in the *Our Boys*, where it delighted my boyish eyes, but that was all I remembered. I mentioned the matter, or Patrick Lagan did, in the column and Seán O'Luineachain of Carrigtuohill came to my rescue. He told me that he had snipped the poem with many others by Denis A. Mac-Carthy, from the *Our Boys* of the 1930s. There were such pleasant affable masterpieces as 'The Tailor that Came from Mayo' and 'The Old Schoolmaster':

Don't you remember old Anthony Cassidy?
Sure, and you must.
Man! But 'twas he had the mental capacity,
Hadn't he just?
How he could argue a case categorical,
Roll out the wonderful word metaphorical,
Talk for whole hours at a stretch like an oracle,
When he discussed.

Seán O'Luineachain told me that from the files of the old *Our Boys* he drew all the honeyed pleasure of recalling boyhood. He said: 'I remember a series of articles even earlier still in the *Our Boys*, which I was too young to value at the time, and I often wonder were they ever published subsequently in more permanent form. They were "The Adventures of the White Arrow".'

And well I remembered them myself. The author was a Mrs Pender who wrote a fine novel called *The Green Cockade*. but I don't think the White Arrow stories were ever collected between the covers of one book. If that is so, then more's the pity. They told of the doings of a lot of brave young fellows, Garrett Og MacArt, Rory the Runner and others in the days of Owen Roe O'Neill. Their com- pany I enjoyed with that of Richard Tyrrell of Tyrrellspass, and as I rode by Granard Moat.

We're almost there. Just a few more echoes and a few more twist of the road ...

There's a plane up there somewhere coming in over the sea and heading over Waterford and Wexford. And I am back in 1912 when Corbett-Wilson made his famous flight from Wales to Ireland. Nobody nowadays would write a poem about such a commonplace effort. Nobody would look up if he heard the noise of an engine overhead. But eighty odd years ago it was a wonder. And I myself am old enough to remember when Scott's Flying Circus toured the country, and based for a while on Strathroy Holm near Omagh Town, and most of us thought that the end of the world had come. Most of us. But not We All. For there were the few, or maybe more, who knew that it was not an end but a beginning.

In 1956 Leo McAdams read an authoritative paper on the Corbett-Wilson flight to the Kilkenny Archaeological Society. And a man in Belgrave Road in Birmingham, who was in Enniscorthy on the day of the flight, wrote a letter to Patrick Lagan. That man's memory of seeing the plane going past at forty miles an hour and at about eight hundred feet was still vivid:

It caused great excitement even among the crows of a local rookery. It was about sundown and like the crows he came in from the South-West.

He lowered himself in three anti-clockwise ellipses of mean diameter of three-quarters of a mile. His final three-quarters included a skim over the top of Vinegar Hill and the same over the spire of the Cathedral and then to the touchdown in the Showgrounds. A repeat occurred about six o'clock on a Sunday morning. Surely Corbett-Wilson liked Enniscorthy. It tested his skill.

And it was a Kilkenny poet, P. Connor of Prospect Park, who wrote two poems on the achievement of Corbett-Wilson. This is one of them:

'Twas on the twenty-third of May, and in the afternoon,
That Mr Corbett-Wilson went up to see the moon.
Right well he done when he began, with courage bold and true,
He soon was far above us from the field of Ardaloo.

The field was a splendid one, no better could be found.
And I was told by many it was once a polo ground.
But never cold the stick and ball nor man with helmet blue,
Bring half the crowd that cheered so loud that day at Ardaloo.

'Twas half-past three when I arrived, the place it seemed alive.
But I was sorry when I heard He could not fly till five.
I roamed about from field to field, I had nothing else to do
But wait to see that splendid flight that day at Ardaloo.

I went down to the hangar, or rather to the nest
Where this great bird was covered up and peacefully at rest.
The canvas soon was taken off to let us have a view
Of that great machine that ne'er was seen before at Ardaloo.

At last 'twas wheeled out to the field amidst a silent throng.
All eyes were fixed upon it as it quickly raced along.
It gradually just ascended, just like a big cuckoo,
And flew for miles around us that day at Ardaloo.

Some people murmured: 'If he fell ...' And some said, 'Ah, No.'
While life and pluck with him remain he'll always give a show.
For none but Him who rules the Earth, and can the storms subdue,
Could share the nerve of that brave man that day at Ardaloo.

Kilkenny always held its own with all that came the way,
But now with Mr Wilson it proudly takes the sway.
You know he is the first great man that o'er the Channel flew,
And landed down in Wexford not far from Ardaloo.

Long life to Mr Wilson may his courage never fail.
May one hundred years pass over e'er his coffin needs a nail.
May God Above protect him and bring him safely through
To give us all another show some day at Ardaloo.

The kindly wish of the last verse was not, alas, to be granted. For the brave aviator went to World War I to be the first man of the British Flying Corps to die in aerial combat.

Did he ever, I wonder, in all his circling go north a bit more and circle over Sweet Avondale where the ghost of Parnell still walks? That errant thought brings back to my memory, and my ears, the sweet voice of my friend Margaret O'Reilly of Gowna singing about the Blackbird of Sweet Avondale. Margaret was known as the Queen of the Ballads. From the threshold of her home, where I often had the happiness of standing with her, you could look down on the beauty of Loch Gowna and over a fair stretch of North Longford.

Margaret, I would say, sang like the birds from the moment she was able to sing and she could have filled a barrel with the medals she won, here, there and everywhere – ever since the great Dr Ben Galligan of Cavan town (he was a good friend of mine) heard her singing and set her on the road to the appropriate places.

Here I look at a letter she wrote me years ago, sending with it the words of 'The Blackbird'. Of the song she said: 'The first verse of this song is the Blackbird Parnell. The other two verses belong to another song also called The Blackbird.' And here it is:

> Ye bold defenders of dear old Erin
> Come pay attention to what I say.
> With pen and paper I will endeavour
> To praise our leader in a simple way.
> Here in Rathdrum, in the County Wicklow,
> This bold defender of Grainne Uaile
> First turned his notes in tones melodious
> Around the lovely woodlands of Avondale.
>
> By the bright Bay of Dublin, while carelessly strolling,
> I sat myself down by a clear crystal steam.
> Reclined on the beach, where the wild waves were rolling,
> In sorrow, condoling, I spied a fair maid
> Her robes changed to mourning that once were so glorious.
> I stood in amazement to hear her sad tale.
> Her heart strings burst forth, in wild accents deploring,
> Saying: 'Where is my Blackbird of Sweet Avondale?'
>
> To the fair counties Meath, Kerry, Cork and Tipperary,
> The notes of his country my blackbird will sing,
> But woe to the hour we'll part light and airy,
> He flew from my arms in Dublin to Ring.
> Now the birds in the forest for me have no charm,
> Not even the voice of the sweet nightingale,
> Her notes though so charming set my poor heart alarming
> Since I lost my poor Blackbird of Sweet Avondale.

There are other versions, God and Parnell know. But that is the one that I heard sung by Margaret O'Reilly of Gowna. To whom once, in the town of Mullingar, which some fine people say is the centre of Ireland, I once read out all the words of this poem. The man who wrote it, whoever he was, was certainly convinced that he belonged to the Centre and every poet is entitled to praise his hometown. So listen:

And Back to Tyrrellspass

AN ODE IN PRAISE OF THE CITY OF MULLINGAR

You may strain your muscles to brag of Brussels,
Of London, Paris or Timbuctoo,
Constantinople or Sebastople,
Vienna, Naples or Tongataboo,
Of Copenhagen, Madrid, Kilbeggan,
Or the Capital of the Russian Czar,
But they're all inferior to the vast superior
And gorgeous city of Mullingar.

That fair metropolis, so great and populous,
Adorns the regions of sweet Westmeath,
That fertile county which Nature's bounty
Has richly gifted with bog and heath.
Them scenes so charming where snipes a-swarming
Attract the sportsmen that come from afar,
And whoever wishes may catch fine fishes
In deep Lough Owel near Mullingar.

I could stay forever by Brosna's River
And watch its waters in their sprarkling fall,
And the ganders swimmin' and lightly skimmin'
O'er the crystal bosom of the Royal Canal.
Or on Thursdays wander 'mid pigs so tender,
And geese and turkeys on many a car,
Exchanging pleasantry with fine bold peasantry
That throng the market at Mullingar.

Ye Nine inspire me and with rapture fire me
To sing the buildings both old and new:
The majestic Courthouse and the spacious Workhouse,
And the Church and steeple which adorn the view.
Then there's barracks airy for the military
Where the brave repose from the toils of war,
Five schools, a nunnery, and a thrivin' tannery
In this gorgeous city of Mullingar.

The railway station with admiration,
I next must mention in terms of praise,
Where trains a-rowlin' and ingines howlin'
Strike each beholder with wild amaze.

And there is Main Street, that broad and clane street,
With its rows of gas-lamps that shine afar.
I could spake a lecture on the architecture
Of the gorgeous city of Mullingar.
The men of genius, contemporaneous,

Approach spontaneous this favoured spot
Where good society and great variety
Of entertainment is still their lot.
The neighbouring Quality for hospitality
And conviviality unequallled are.
And from December until November
There's still diversion in Mullingar.

Now, in conclusion, I make allusion
To the beauteous females that here abound:
Celestial creatures with lovely features
And taper ankles that skim the ground.
But this suspends me, the theme transcends me.
My Muse's powers are too weak by far.
It would need Catullus, likewise Tibullus,
To sing the praise of Mullingar.

And from the wonders of Mullingar we pass on to Granard
Moat and the memory of Tyrrell of Tyrrellspass. We do it
with the aid of *The Ballads of Ireland: Collected and Edited with
Notes Historical and Biographical* by Edward Hayes.

The Baron bold of Trimbleston hath gone, in proud array,
To drive afar from fair Westmeath the Irish kerns away.
And there is mounting brisk of steeds and donning shirts of mail,
And spurring hard to Mullingar 'mong Riders of the Pale.

For, flocking round his banner there, from east to west there came,
Full many knights and gentlemen of English blood and name,
All prompt to hate the Irish race, all spoilers of the land,
And mustered soon a thousand spears that Baron in his band.

For trooping in rode Nettervilles and D'Altons not a few,
And thick as reeds pranced Nugent's spears, a fierce and godless crew;
And Nagle's pennon flutters fair, and pricking o'er the plain,
Dashed Tuite of Somna's mail-clad men, and Dillon's from Glenshane.

And Back to Tyrrellspass

A goodly feast the Baron gave in Nagle's ancient hall,
And to his board he summons there his chiefs and captains all;
And round the red wine circles fast, with noisy boast and brag,
How they would hunt the Irish kerns like any Cratloe stag.

But 'mid their glee a horseman spurr'd all breathless to the gate,
And from the warder there he crav'd to see Lord Barnwell straight;
And when he stept the castle hall, then cried the Baron, 'Ho!
You are De Petit's body-squire, why stops your master so?'

'Sir Piers De Petit ne'er held back' that wounded man replied,
'When friend or foeman called him on, or there was need to ride;
But vainly now you lack him here, for, on the bloody sod,
The noble knight lies stark and stiff – his soul is with his God.

'For yesterday, in passing through Fertullah's wooded glen,
Fierce Tyrrell met my master's band, and slew the good knight then;
And, wounded sore with axe and skian, I barely 'scaped with life,
To bear to you the dismal news, and warn you of the strife.

'MacGeoghegan's flag is on the hills! O'Reilly's up at Fore!
And all the chiefs have flown to arms, from Allen to Donore,
And as I rode by Granard moat, right plainly might I see
O'Ferall's clans were sweeping down from distant Annalee.'

Then started up young Barnwell there, all hot with Spanish wine –
'Revenge,' he cries, 'for Petit's death, and be that labour mine;
I'll hunt to death the rebel bold, and hang him on a tree!'

Then rose a shout throughout the hall that made the rafters ring,
And stirr'd o'erhead the banners there, like aspen leaves in spring;
And vows were made, and wine-cups quaft, with proud and bitter scorn,
To hunt to death Fertullah's clans upon the coming morn.

These tidings unto Tyrrell came, upon that selfsame day,
Where, camped amid the hazel boughs, he at Lough Ennel lay.
'And they will hunt us so,' he cried – 'why, let them if they will;
But first we'll teach them greenwood craft, to catch us, ere they kill.'

And hot next morn the horsemen came, Young Barnwell at their head;
But when they reached the calm lake banks, behold! their prey was fled!
And loud they cursed, as wheeling round they left that tranquil shore,
And sought the wood of Garraclune, and searched it o'er and o'er.

And as I Rode by Granard Moat

And down the slopes, and o'er the fields, and up the steeps they strain,
And through Moylanna's trackless bog; where many steeds remain,
Till wearied all, at set of sun, they halt in sorry plight,
And on the heath, beside his steed, each horseman passed the night.

Next morn, while yet the white mists lay, all brooding on the hill,
Bold Tyrrell to his comrade spake, a friend in every ill –
'O'Conor, take ye ten score men, and speed ye to the dell,
Where winds the path to Kinnegad – you know that togher well.

'And couch ye close amid the heath, and blades of waving fern,
So glint of steel, or glimpse of man, no Saxon may discern,
Until ye hear my bugle blown, and up O'Conor, then,
And bid the drums strike Tyrrell's march, and charge ye with your men.'

'Now by his soul who sleeps at Cong,' O'Conor proud replied,
'It grieves me sore, before those dogs, to have my head to hide;
But lest, perchance, in scorn they might go brag it thro' the Pale,
I'll do my best that few shall live to carry round the tale.'

The mist roll'd off, and 'Gallants up!' young Barnwell loudly cries,
'By Bective's shrine, from off the hill, the rebel traitor flies;
Now mount ye all, fair gentlemen – lay bridle loose on mane,
And spur your steeds with rowels sharp – we'll catch him on the plain.'

Then bounded to their saddles quick a thousand eager men,
And on they rushed in hot pursuit to Darra's wooded glen.
But gallants bold, tho' fair ye ride, here slacken speed ye may –
The chase is o'er! – the hunt is up! – the quarry stands at bay!

For, halted on a gentle slope, bold Tyrrell placed his hand,
And proudly stept he to the front, his banner in his hand,
And plung'd it deep within the earth, all plainly in their view,
And waved aloft his trusty sword, and loud his bugle blew.

Saint Colman! 'twas a fearful sight, while drum and trumpet played,
To see the bound from out the brake that fierce O'Conor made,
As waving high his sword in air he smote the flaunting crest
Of proud Sir Hugh de Geneville, and clove him to the chest!

'On comrades, on!' young Barnwell cries, 'and spur ye to the plain,
Where we may best our lances use!' That counsel is in vain.
For down swept Tyrrell's gallant band, with shout and wild halloo,
And a hundred steeds are masterless since first his bugle blew!

And Back to Tyrrellspass

From front to flank the Irish charge in battle order all,
While pent like sheep in shepherd's fold the Saxon riders fall;
Their lances long are little use, their numbers block the way,
And mad with pain their plunging steeds add terror to the fray!

And of the haughty host that rode that morning through the dell,
But one has 'scaped with life and limb his comrades' fate to tell;
The rest all in their harness died, amid the thickets there,
Yet fighting to the latest gasp, like foxes in a snare!

The Baron bold of Trimbleston has fled in sore dismay,
Like beaten hound at dead of night from Mullingar away,
While wild from Boyne to Brusna's banks there spreads a voice of wail,
Mavrone! the sky that night was red with burnings in the Pale!

And late next day to Dublin town the dismal tidings came,
And Kevin's-Port and Watergate are lit with beacons twain,
And scouts spur out, and on the walls there stands a fearful crowd,
While high o'er all Saint Mary's bell tolls out alarums loud!

But far away beyond the Pale, from Dunluce to Dunboy,
From every Irish hall and rath there bursts a shout of joy,
As eager Asklas hurry past o'er mountain, moor, and glen,
And tell in each the battle won by Tyrrell and his men.

And tomorrow we may set out from Granard nor make any stop until we get to Omagh or Claramore or Ultima Thule.

Some years ago when I was making a journey to the handsome town of Tyrrellspass I was set to thinking on the landed gentleman who locked up his wife for years and years because she would not sell her jewels (to which he had no legal right) and give him the proceeds.

You'll find the reflection of that overly possessive husband in Maria Edgeworth's novel *Castle Rackrent*, when the impoverished Sir Kit Rackrent marries in London a rich Jewish heiress and brings her back with him to Ireland hoping to benefit by her wealth. When she refuses to be used in such a scurvy fashion, he locks her up and keeps her locked up until he himself meets an untimely end in a duel, and the lady is happily released.

Maria Edgeworth herself thought that her readers, some of them, might not credit the story so she told in a footnote the true story on which it was based, the story of what she called the 'conjugal imprisonment' of Lady Cathcart. During her imprisonment her husband was visited quite regularly by the local gentry, and Maria wrote that it was his custom at dinner to send his compliments to his wife, telling her that the company had the honour to drink her health, and asking her if there was anything at table she would like to eat. Her answer always was: 'Lady Cathcart's compliments, and she has every thing she wants.'

Her diamonds she had successfully hidden from her husband but there was neither servant nor friend to whom she could entrust them. She had noticed from her window a beggarwoman who came to the house and one day she called to her, threw her the parcel of diamonds and gave her the name of the person to whom she should deliver them. Years later, when Lady Cathcart was freed and her husband dead, she received her jewels safely. Miss Edgeworth was much impressed by that instance of the honesty of the Irish poor and, indeed, she had good reason to be.

Twenty years the poor lady was locked up and it was said that on the day of her liberation she had scarcely the clothes to cover her. She wore a red wig, looked scared and stupefied and said that she scarcely knew one person from another.

That story came back into my mind when, years ago, on the journey to Tyrrellspass I read an historical and archaeological appreciation of the place by Dr Peter Harbison, prepared specially for that visit – not specially for me, but for a party led by Eamonn Ceannt, then General Director of Bórd Fáilte.

Dr Harbison had been writing about Jane, Countess of Belvedere, to whose credit must be laid the original planning and architectural achievement of Tyrrellspass. And he mentioned also that an earlier Countess of the same name had been locked up for twenty years because of the jealousy of her husband.

Howandever: Tyrrellspass, which already had the bones and many of the habiliments of beauty, had, at the time of that journey, been selected by Bórd Fáilte for special attention during an Architectural Heritage Year: to restore ancient buildings and monuments, brighten the face of the place, remove the blemishes left there by what we laughingly call modern living. The work was splendidly done and we come now to a vision of a place that I first dreamed of in the late 1920s when I read about Tyrrell of Tyrrellspass and debated history with Paddy McCillion in my Aunt Kate's great farmhouse at Claramore by Drumquin in West Tyrone ...

Acknowledgments

The publisher has made every effort to acquire all the permissions needed, and would be glad to hear from any copyright-holders who have not been included. For kind permission to reprint copyright material The Lilliput Press gratefully acknowledges the following:

Maurice James Craig for 'Ballad to a Traditional Refrain' and 'Georgian Dublin'; Oliver D. Gogarty for 'Leda and the Swan' by Oliver St John Gogarty; the Trustees of the Estate of Patrick Kavanagh, c/o Peter Fallon, Literary Agent, Loughcrew, Old-castle, Co. Meath, for 'Renewal', 'Canal Bank Walk', 'Spraying the Potatoes', 'A Christmas Childhood' and 'Lines Written on a Seat on the Grand Canal' by Patrick Kavanagh; Margaret Farrington and Elizabeth Ryan for 'Aodh Ruadh Ó Domhnaill' by Thomas MacGreevy; David Hammond for 'Wild Slieve Gallen Brae'; David Higham Associates for 'Train to Dublin' and 'The Closing Album: Dublin' by Louis MacNeice (from *Collected Poems*, Faber and Faber); the author and The Gallery Press for 'Like Dolmens Round My Childhood, the Old People' and 'A Lost Tradition' by John Montague (from *Collected Poems*); Francis Stuart for 'A Racehorse at the Curragh; A.P. Watt Ltd of London on behalf of Michael Yeats for 'The Pilgrim' and 'A Prayer for My Daughter' by W.B. Yeats (from *The Collected Poems*, Macmillan); Anne B. Yeats for the cover drawing by Jack B. Yeats, 'A Sligo Ballad Singer'.

The Lilliput Press would like to thank W.J. Mc Cormack, Susan Schreibman, Peter Sirr and Jonathan Williams for their assistance in locating copyright-holders, and Vincent Hurley and Máire Kennedy for their bibliographical help.